DANGEROUS ENGLISH!

An Indispensable Guide for Language Learners and Others

by Elizabeth Claire

Pictures by Dave Nicholson and eluki bes shahar

PUBLISHING FOR ONE WORLD

NEW AGE INTERNATIONAL (P) LIMITED, PUBLISHERS

(formerly Wiley Eastern Limited)

New Delhi • Bangalore • Chennai • Cochin • Guwahati • Hyderabad
Jalandhar • Kolkata • Lucknow • Mumbai • Ranchi

Visit us at www.newagepublishers.com

Third Edition
by Elizabeth Claire

ISBN 81-224-1635-7
2 3 4 5 6 7 8 9 10
C-05-07-211

Indian Price 125/-
Original Price $ 10.95

Printed in India at Sanjeev Offset

PUBLISHING FOR ONE WORLD
NEW AGE INTERNATIONAL (P) LIMITED, PUBLISHERS
(formerly Wiley Eastern Ltd.)

New Delhi • Bangalore • Chennai • Cochin • Guwahati • Hyderabad
Jalandhar • Kolkata • Lucknow • Mumbai • Ranchi
Visit us at www.newagepublishers.com

About Dangerous English

Dangerous English! is the third edition of the now-classic *Dangerous English! An Indispensable Guide for Language Learners and Others.* This latest edition has been entirely revised, updated, and expanded. While there are many new dangers in the English language, we feel that the climate is no longer too dangerous to openly discuss these language features in the classroom. With this in mind, each chapter contains suggestions for increased linguistic awareness, plus discussion questions. There is an expanded teachers' section at the end of the book.

Other new features:

- All definitions and sample sentences have been brought up to date.
- New dangerous words have been added, out-of-use words have been deleted.
- The pronunciation key is now more useful–international phonetic alphabet.
- The reading level has been lowered–shorter sentences, simpler grammar.
- There is additional attention to formal terms, including vocabulary for sexually transmitted diseases.
- There are more illustrations to help clarify meanings.
- The current movie and TV rating systems are explained.

Additional topics are covered:

- The cultural origins of American taboos
- Sexual harassment
- Changes in English reflecting changes in society
- The new taboos: politically incorrect terms
- Euphemisms for unpleasant facts of life
- True stories of Dangerous English

Acknowledgments

This exciting new edition would not have been possible without the contributions of many people.

I'd like to especially thank the world's foremost authority on dangerous words in any language, Dr. Reinhold Aman, editor of *Maledicta, The International Journal of Verbal Aggression*. The scholarship and research in his journal, plus the lengthy interviews he granted me, provided a foundation for a sizable portion of this book. Thank you, Rey, for your generous and knowledgeable assistance.

Thanks to Dick Patchin of Delta Systems for his courageous promotion and marketing of this text, making it available at a modest cost to the many new speakers of English who need it.

Special thanks to Jeff Weingarten, René, Jon Sicherman, Steve Jorgensen, James Manzella, and many anonymous others for knowing words I don't know, picking through the words, and checking local usages and meanings.

Thanks to George A. Rowland for his eagle eye and careful scholarship in editing, as well as for his clever wit, which provided the only exercise I got while doing this revision: belly laughs.

To Joe Frazier go thanks for his exciting rendition of our cover design; to Dave Nicholson for the playful art to complement eluki bes shahar's classic drawings for the original *Dangerous English!*

Thanks to Brenda Cianci for her integrity and sunshine in the office each day and to Kimberly Vuz for a careful reading of the manuscript, picking up the last unclosed parentheses and undotted i's.

Thanks to Stephanie Stauffer for transcribing the phonetic pronunciations.

To Geoff Hill for technological support and computer expertise.

To Jeannie Patchin for her expert eyes in the final edit.

My great appreciation goes to Linda Bruell for design and execution of pages, pictures, and IPA transcriptions and miraculous patience with the nitpicking details of getting the work ready for printing.

About the Author

In our 1990 edition, among many other things, we said: "Believe it or not, Elizabeth Claire is a mild-mannered grandmother residing in Saddle Brook, New Jersey. She received her Master's Degree in TESOL from New York University. Elizabeth has taught English as a Second Language for twenty-four years to students of all ages, and wrote the original edition of *Dangerous English!* because she was too embarrassed to explain terms she knew her students wanted and needed. When, in 1980, no publishing company was willing to take the risk of publishing this guide, she borrowed money from her even milder-mannered mother to produce and market the work that has since become a "classic in the field." All of that is still true (now thirty years' experience) except for the mild-mannered part. When Elizabeth ran for public office in her town, rumors about her authorship of *Dangerous English!* got translated into the opposition's contention that she wrote pornographic novels. (She might have lost anyway; we'll never know.) She is the founder and editor of *Easy English NEWS* as well as the author of twenty other texts and resources for people learning English. She stands for creating a peaceful planet on which language is used, not to put down, insult, or start wars, but to generate cooperation, fun, and aliveness.

Dangerous English! has been translated into Chinese, Japanese, and Polish.

Among Elizabeth Claire's other works are:

Three Little Words: A, An, and The
(An Indispensable Guide to English Articles)
What's So Funny?
(An Introduction to American Humor)
The ESL Teacher's Activities Kit
The ESL Teacher's Holiday Activities Kit
The ESL Wonder Workbooks:
 # 1 All About Me and # 2 All Around Me
JUST-A-MINUTE! An Oral Language-Learning Game
Classroom Teacher's ESL Survival Kit # 1 (with Judie Haynes)
Classroom Teacher's ESL Survival Kit #2 (with Judie Haynes)
The Where Is Taro? ESL Program: "A novel approach"

Contents

To the Reader

In every culture there are topics and words that are dangerous. That means that educated people do not talk about these taboo topics and do not use these taboos in polite company.

Are you a new speaker of English? Do you worry about being embarrassed for saying the wrong thing at the wrong time?

Are you curious about the way Americans speak outside of the office or the classroom?

Dangerous English 2000! was written to help you!

What Makes Some Words Dangerous?

Words are just combinations of sounds. But parents, teachers, religious leaders, and sacred books teach us not to say some of those combinations. This censorship makes these words emotionally charged. The taboo is usually passed down from generation to generation. New words are invented to take the place of the forbidden ones. Sometimes these new words become taboo, too.

In the past thirty years, there have been many social changes in the United States. Taboo words are now often accepted where they were never heard before–in many social groups, among women, and in the media. But there still are places where the words are generally *not* welcome: in school and houses of worship, in many offices, in formal meetings and parties of mixed ages and genders, and in the presence of older people or children.

What topics are taboo for Americans?

Among the topics that Americans don't talk about in formal situations (except at the doctor's office) are:

- sexual parts of our bodies
- sexual activities
- bathroom functions
- excrement
- disgusting things such as vomit and nose picking
- upsetting things such as cancer, death, and dying

Americans also advise each other to avoid discussing religion, politics, and racial issues because these may lead to arguments over differences of opinion.

What words are taboo?

Dr. Reinhold Aman, an expert on "maledicta" (bad words), explains three kinds of taboo words: obscenities, blasphemies, and slurs.

Obscenities are vulgar words for sexual body parts, sexual acts, and excrement. A few hundred years ago, these words were used freely, and were not taboo. Examples: *cock*, *fuck*, *shit*.

Blasphemy is language that religious teachings say are taboo: *God damn it*; *go to Hell*; *Jesus Christ!* These words may be used in a religious context, but not for other reasons.

Slurs are insulting words about someone's nationality or race. Some words for racial or national groups are among the most dangerous words in the language: *kike*, *wop*, *nigger*.

Why are these topics and words taboo in the U.S.?

Taboos have beginnings (and in some cases, endings). At some point in history, a group of people declared that a word or a topic was taboo. If the group was influential, the taboo was circulated and passed on to the rest of the society.

English-speaking society in America began in the early 1600's. Immigrants from England came here in order to have freedom to practice their own form of religion. These Puritans, Separatists, and other fundamental Christians had very strict ideas about sex: Sex was for creating children. Sex for other reasons was a sin (a crime against God). The churches taught that anything that reminded people of sex should be covered, both from their eyes and from their ears. The words that people used for physical acts became taboo.

Today, almost four hundred years later, Americans are still influenced by this early history. In general, Americans are the most puritanical people in the world when it comes to talking about naked bodies, sex, and bathroom activities. These topics make most of them uncomfortable.

The Bible is the Christian holy book. Part of it is based on Jewish Scriptures. It teaches that God forbids people to say His name "in vain" or for a worthless reason. It is a sin to blaspheme–to insult God.

America has had a long history of cruel race relations. From 1619 to 1863, many white landowners (especially in the southern states) kept Africans as slaves. The slaves were freed following a bloody civil war between the North and the South. A hundred years after the war black people were just beginning to gain full civil rights, including the right to vote in all states.

During the same time, Native Americans (Indians) lost many battles with Americans and with the U.S. government. Their populations died from disease and hunger as well as in battle.

Relations between the white and black, and the white and red, races have improved; however, there are still many areas of pain, distrust, and dislike. Many of the names that people call people of another group are derogatory and offensive. The terms are taboo among thoughtful people who don't want to hurt others. The word *nigger* recalls great cruelty and oppression. Among white people, it is perhaps the most taboo word in American English.

People from many ethnic groups have immigrated to the United States. Groups could not understand each other because of different languages. Many of the names that people in one group called other groups were derogatory.

People who are different from the people in power often have fewer legal rights and fewer social opportunities. In addition to people of other races, this includes: women, homosexuals, disabled people, people with different physical features, children, the elderly, fat, short, and poor people. Many of the names for them are derogatory.

What is the power of taboo words?

When a word may not be said in most ordinary, everyday situations (school, business or family life), it acquires a special and mysterious power.

Teenagers use taboo words to sound "cool," and to rebel against parents and school rules. Shouting a taboo word or two helps people to express pain and release anger.

Male groups use taboo social words to create bonds of friendship. Lovers use taboo sex terms to stimulate passion, and comedians use all sorts of taboo words to make people laugh.

Why are there so many words for sex and other taboo topics?

Whatever is taboo is interesting. People spend a good amount of time thinking about and talking about taboo things. In many cases, *euphemisms* (polite words) and *slang* terms (clever, "off-color" words) are substituted for the taboo words. There is only one English common word for shoulder, ear, or knee. But there are hundreds of words for each of our sexual body parts.

How can I recognize that a word is dangerous or taboo?

You can't, unless someone tells you. That's why you need this book.

It is not the *meaning* of the word that makes it dangerous. *Buttocks*, *behind*, and *ass* all mean the same part of the body. *Buttocks* is a "clean" word, used in formal situations; *behind* is a "cleaner" word, used in general conversation; and *ass* is a "dirty" word, used in informal situations, but *avoided* in school, writing, and business. You might ask, what made "*ass*" a bad word, if it is all right to say "*buttocks*" or "*behind*?"

It is not the *sound* of a word that makes it dangerous. For example, *Dick* is a very common name for a man. It is a nickname for Richard. *Dick* (spelled with a small *d*) is also a very common word for penis (the male sex organ). We may talk about a person named *Dick*. But we cannot, in polite company, talk about a penis or a *dick*. *Dick* is a taboo word when it means penis. It is not taboo when it is a person's name.

What if I use taboo words without knowing it?

A good friend will warn you and explain. If you are among strangers–some will smile because they understand that English is new to you. It will make a funny story to tell their friends. Others may think you are uneducated, lower-class, insensitive, immoral, mean, or rude.

Dangerous English can be *very* dangerous. People have even been killed for insults, slurs, and angry foul language they have used.

Dangerous English! will save you from many embarrassing situations. It will help you to understand a very interesting part of American culture. It will keep you safe (in many cases) from other people's disapproval and anger. You need this book. We hope you enjoy it!

Discussion

1. According to Dr. Reinhold Aman, what are three kinds of taboo words?

2. What groups of people and events in history created taboos in language in American English?

3. What taboo topics does your language share with English? What different taboos are in your language? What groups of people or events created the taboos in your language?

4. What "power" does a taboo word have?

5. What taboo words in your language are used when a person hurts himself or herself and gets angry?

6. Why are there so many words for sexual things?

7. How can you tell that a word is taboo?

8. Are there people's names in your native language that are also the names of sex organs or other embarrassing things? Do some people change their names for this reason?

9. Is *your* name a "dangerous" word in English? If it is, what do you think you will do about it?

Is Your Pronunciation Dangerous?

Do you have trouble pronouncing some English sounds?

If you are a new speaker of English, this is not surprising. English has forty-four sounds, while many other languages have only twenty-five or thirty sounds. English words may have two or three consonants in a row, while languages such as Spanish, Italian, and Japanese have vowels between each consonant. Our tongues have difficulty pronouncing sounds that they did not learn before the age of thirteen.

Sometimes these difficulties can be embarrassing. A *mis*pronunciation can change an innocent word into a dangerous word!

There are twenty-three different vowel sounds. Almost all new speakers have *some* difficulty hearing and pronouncing many of them. For example, it's difficult for speakers of Chinese, French, Greek, Italian, Japanese, Spanish and many other languages to hear a difference between /iː/ ("long *e*"), as in *heat*, from /ɪ/ ("short *i*"), as in *hit*. They may pronounce both words nearly the same. When someone says, "I'm going to hit the water," we may not be sure of what he or she means.

"I'm going to hit the water."

Test your pronunciation

Have a native English speaker read the following pairs of words to you. Can you hear the difference, or do they sound the same? Next, have the English speaker listen as *you* say the words. Do *you* say them correctly?

sick, seek	did, deed	fill, feel	pill, peel
sin, seen	chip, cheap	lip, leap	still, steal
ship, sheep			

If you had trouble with these pairs of words, watch out!

This pronunciation problem means that when you want to say *sheet* (a cloth covering for a bed), you may be saying *shit* (a vulgar word for feces).

When you want to say *piece* (a part of), it may sound like *piss* (passing urine into the toilet).

This mispronunciation can sound very funny to Americans, and may be embarrassing to you.

"I put some clean shits on the bed."

If you want to say this:		Don't say this!	
beach	(biːtʃ)	bitch	(bɪtʃ)
piece	(piːs)	piss	(pɪs)
sheet	(ʃiːt)	shit	(ʃɪt)

"Do you mind if I take a piss?"

Other vowel sounds can cause troubles, too:

If you want to say this:		Don't say this!	
six	(sɪks)	sex	(sɛks)
fork	(fɔːrk)	fuck	(fʌk)
folks	(fouks)	fucks	(fʌks)
fox	(fɑks)	fucks	(fʌks)
slot	(slɑt)	slut	(slʌt)
Kirk	(kəːrk)	cock	(kɑk)
her	(həːr)	whore	(hɔːr)
can't	(kænt)	cunt	(kʌnt)

Do you have trouble with the /th/ sounds (θ) and (ð)? They are difficult for almost all people who learn English after the age of thirteen. This is because the sounds do not exist in most other languages.

Here's how to pronounce /θ/ correctly: Stick out your tongue just a little bit between your upper teeth and your lower teeth. Gently force air from your mouth out between your tongue and your upper teeth. For /ð/ do the same, but use your vocal cords at the same time.

If you want to say this:		Don't say this!	
third	(θərd)	turd	(tərd)
farther	('fɑːr ðər)	farter	('fɑːrt er)
teeth	(tiːθ)	teat	(tiːt)
theses	('θiː siːs)	feces	('fiː siːz)

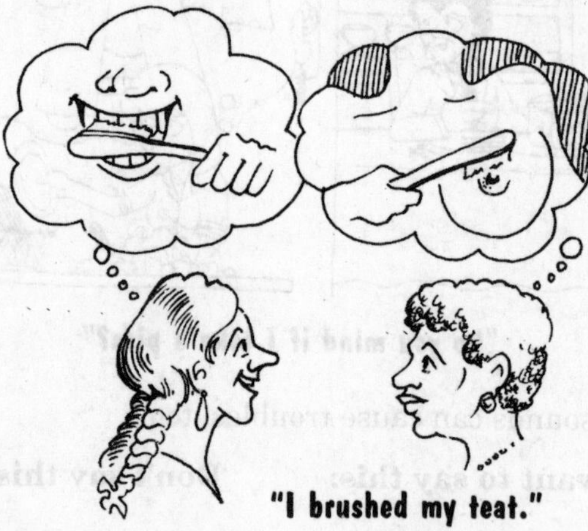

"I brushed my teat."

Are you from Japan or China? Or some other place in Asia? Some Asian languages have only one sound where English has two: /l/ and /r/.
This makes it very hard for you to make an English /l/ or /r/ that sounds right to Americans.

If you want to say this:		Don't say this!	
ray	(rei)	lay	(lei)
rust	(rʌst)	lust	(lʌst)
rude	(ruːd)	lewd	(luːd)
lump	(lʌmp)	rump	(rʌmp)
clap	(klæp)	crap	(kræp)
elect	(ə 'lɛkt)	erect	(ə 'rɛkt)
election	(ə 'lɛk ʃən)	erection	(ə 'rɛk ʃən)
blessed	(blɛst)	breast	(brɛst)

There are many jokes about the way that Asians pronounce English l's and r's. This isn't polite, of course, but the mistakes just sound funny to American ears. Especially when dangerous words result.

A common thing to say to a friend who is running for election to any club office or public office: "Lots of luck on your coming election." But to make a joke, the well-wisher will fold his hands in front of him and bow, as though he were Japanese. He will imitate a Japanese accent. Then he will say this: "Rots of ruck on your coming erection." The deliberate mispronunciation usually makes people smile.

"The audience crapped for a long time after the concert."

"Rots of ruck on your coming erection."

Speakers of Arabic, Japanese, Greek, Korean, Spanish and Tagalog sometimes confuse the sound /v/ with /b/.

If you want to say this:		**Don't say this!**	
vowel	(vauəl)	bowel	(baʊəl)

Vietnamese, Korean, Chinese and others may have trouble with the sound /b/ in initial position:

If you want to say this:		**Don't say this!**	
bee	(biː)	pee	(piː)
Mr. Becker	('bɛ kər)	Mr. Pecker	('pɛ kər)
brick	(brɪk)	prick	(prɪk)

Many Asians, especially Koreans and some Japanese, have difficulty with the /s/ sound before an /ɪ/ (short *i*) sound. Watch out!

If you want to say this:		**Don't say this!**	
city	('sɪt i)	shitty	('ʃɪt i)
Please sit down (sɪt daʊn)		Please shit down (ʃɪt daʊn)	
university (yu nɪ 'vər sɪt i)		univershitty (yu nɪ 'vər ʃɪt i)	

Do you have any of these pronunciation problems? We hope that you will now see how important it can be to correct them!

Discussion

1. Have you had any embarrassing experiences because of your accent?

2. What is the best way to avoid these dangerous mispronunciations?

3. What dangerous mispronunciations do Americans or other English speakers use when they learn your native language?

The Social Classes of English Words

An English word has a sound, a spelling, and one or more meanings. Words for taboo topics also have a *"social class."* This means that a word is acceptable in one or more social settings. When a word is used in a different setting, it is out of place. It may be offensive or embarrassing.

In this book, we'll talk about six social classes of words.

formal	**children's words**
general use	**slang**
euphemism	**vulgar**

Formal words. These are the words in biology textbooks and the words doctors use. Use formal words whenever you want to be clear and exact. Both men and women use formal words. Young people and uneducated people may not know the formal terms for sexual parts of their bodies.

General use. These words are the best-known and most commonly used by American men and women. They are clear in their meanings. A formal word may also be in general use.

Euphemism ('yu fə mɪ zm). A euphemism is a "polite" word. It is less clear than a formal or general use word, but the meaning is usually understood. Euphemisms are the safest words for the foreign student to use. Americans commonly use euphemisms in conversation with people they don't know very well, with older people, and in mixed groups of both men and women. The universal euphemisms are expressions like "you-know-what" or "you-know-where."

Personal euphemisms. A family or a group of friends may invent words about sex or bathroom activities. They use these personal euphemisms when they are having a conversation in a public place. They do not want other people to know what they are talking about.

Children's words. Many parents use special words with children. These are easy for the children to pronounce when they are learning to talk. Later, special euphemisms may be used with children. Occasionally, adults may use children's words or "baby talk" to be funny.

Slang is used in informal situations where a person feels comfortable with friends or associates. Slang words often are new words in the language, or old words that now have a new meaning. If the word becomes popular and people use it for many years, it may come into general use.

Slang words may have "an attitude." That is, the word can show the speaker's feelings or opinion about something. Many slang expressions show creativity, humor, affection, hostility, anger, or resentment. Some slang terms are *derogatory* (də 'ra gə tʊ riː). Derogatory words are offensive. Americans may use derogatory words and not know that they are offensive to the people they are talking to (or about).

The word chair does not contain an opinion about the *object* chair. But the slang word *broad* (which means *woman*) includes an attitude about women. The attitude comes from the history of how the word has been used. Men have used the word *broad* when they have talked about women as though women have no brains or personalities. Most women find this attitude offensive, and so the *word* is offensive.

The words you speak may also speak about you. They tell other people about your attitudes and prejudices. You might not know that this is happening. For example, a man who refers to women as *broads* is telling listeners that his attitude toward women is not respectful.

A person who calls a Spanish speaker a *Spic* is letting people know that he or she is not very sensitive and shows prejudice.

A man who calls a grown woman a *girl* tells people that he thinks of women as child-like.

Things can often become very confusing when offensive words are said with an intention to be funny. The words may then create a friendly bond between speaker and listener. (That is, they will create a bond *if* the listener understands the humorous intention and also finds the words funny.)

Vulgar words are the lowest social class of words. They are the simple, clear words of uneducated people for body parts and sex and bathroom terms. Careful speakers *never* use vulgar words in formal situations, in the classroom, in the office, or in formal written work. Don't use vulgar words when speaking to teachers, superiors, customers, older people, children, strangers, new friends, and mixed groups of both men and women.

Using vulgar language is called *swearing* or *cursing*.

A listener may find some slang and vulgar words offensive. They make him or her feel insulted. This can happen even if the speaker did not intend it.

Vulgar language is often used in such all-male groups as work teams and sports teams, men's college dormitories, the army, bars, and street gangs. Men of every social class from street cleaner to banker, senator and president might use these words. In some settings, men use vulgar words in every sentence. Psychologists say that this is a form of "male bonding." That is, the words are a badge of team membership; they add spice and humor to the language.

In today's age of equality, the women who join some of these formerly all-male groups may use vulgar language, too. Men who use vulgar language freely may consider a woman who also swears at work or in school as "one of the boys." But in a dating relationship, women who don't swear may seem more "classy" to these same men and, therefore, may seem more attractive.

Vulgar sex and toilet words are contained in many other expressions. They are used to express anger, or to act as a weapon. When the word is combined with an angry tone of voice, the intention is to hurt, drive away, punish, or humiliate another person.

Years ago, polite men would never swear when a woman or a child was near. "Watch your language, there are ladies present" was a reminder. Today, young women are not surprised by, and may not even be offended to hear, vulgar language at parties, and even at work. Many women use vulgar language as freely in informal situations as men do. In general, older women know fewer vulgar words than younger women, and use them less frequently. Neither group uses as much vulgar language as men do.

Teenagers may use vulgar language in order to be accepted by their group. Using forbidden words is a way of showing they are "growing up." They dare each other to write vulgar expressions on bathroom walls or buildings.

People with very little education may use vulgar terms for body parts and functions. Such terms have no forbidden feeling for them. They learned them from their parents. In fact, the vulgar terms may be the only words they know for those functions.

Some very-well-educated people prefer to use vulgar terms for the natural functions of the body. They feel that the formal words and euphemisms are prudish. They say that the vulgar words are more honest and direct, and express their feelings more accurately.

There are some people who are shocked and strongly offended by vulgar language. It is against their religious and moral beliefs to use such language. They don't like to hear it. That's a very good reason not to use vulgar language with people you don't know.

When a person with a strong foreign accent uses vulgar expressions in English, it has a comic sound. But that might not be the effect that the speaker wanted.

Discussion

1. What are the *social classes* of English words?

2. When or where would you use formal language? Slang? Vulgar? Children's words? General use? A euphemism?

3. Which is the safest type of word to use in polite company?

4. Are there such classes of words in your native language? Are there additional levels? Are there "men's words" and "women's words"? Children's words?

5. Why is it OK for a man to use a certain word, but dangerous for a woman to use it?

6. What does vulgar language accomplish in male groups?

7. What are men's attitudes about women when they use the same vulgar words?

8. Which classes of words may have an "attitude" or point of view? How does this add to their meaning?

We All Do It, but We Can't Talk about It

We eat food, we digest food in our stomachs, and we pass the undigested part of food out of our bodies.

What shall we call this undigested food?

It depends on where we are and to whom we are talking.

School textbooks might use the term *waste material* in a chapter about digestion. This way, teacher and students can discuss digestion without being embarrassed. "Waste material" is a euphemism. This term does not have a specific, clear meaning. That way the subject matter "doesn't smell bad."

A formal term for waste material is *stool*. This word is used by doctors and patients, and in medical reports: "The patient's stool was watery." "Take your stool sample to the laboratory for testing." "They found blood in his stool."

Feces is also a formal term. It's correct to use this term when you want to be clear and direct with educated people. It may refer to either human or animal waste: "There were mouse feces in the closet; we set a trap to catch the mice." Feces is always used in the plural. There is no singular form.

Fecal matter is a formal, somewhat sterilized (cleaned up) term. It might be used in an inspector's report on a restaurant. The term suggests that it is a small amount: "Fecal matter was found in the canned spaghetti sauce." "A certain amount of insect parts and rodent [rat or mouse] fecal matter is allowed in the food-canning process."

Excrement is a general-use term that includes all types of human and animal feces. It smells bad.

Bowel movement is in general use. This term is all right for talk in the family, or to the doctor: "I haven't had a bowel movement for three days." It's too strong for the neighbors, though.

B.M. (or *b.m.*) This euphemism for bowel movement is less clear, so it is more polite. You can use this term when talking to the neighbors. But only if absolutely necessary. Americans consider bathroom habits to be a very personal subject. Exceptions are made for mothers of small children. B.m.'s, diapers, toilet training, and other bathroom matters relating to their children are an important part of their daily world.

The taboo is also broken if it is necessary to speak of an illness.

Caca is a child's word. So are: *cackee*, *a a*, *eh eh*, *poop*, *poopie*, *poozie doodoo*, and *doody*. These are all easy sounds for a child to say so he or she can tell Mom or Dad when a b.m. is on the way: "I have to make caca"; "I have to go caca"; and so on.

Number two. This euphemism is very common with school-age children: "I have to go to the bathroom." "Do you have to do number one or number two?" "Number two."

Turd is vulgar slang for an individual piece of waste material. It is a commonly used term for human, dog, cat, or bird feces: "He flushed the turds down the toilet." "The park was filled with dog turds." Turd is a *countable* noun. That is, it has both a singular and a plural form.

Droppings is a euphemism for animal excrement. *Horse droppings* are humorously called *road apples*. A cow's waste is politely called *cow droppings*, and humorously called *cow flop*, *cow pancakes*, *pasture patties*, or (when dry) *cow chips*. Cow droppings and horse droppings may be called *dung* or *manure* when they are used as fertilizer.

Dirt is a euphemism for dog or cat feces: "People must clean up their dog's dirt." Signs along the street tell us "Clean up after your dog." They don't have to mention what. *Dog doo* is another euphemism.

Shit is considered vulgar, although this common word used to be acceptable. (That was hundreds of years ago.) Now you won't often hear this word in "polite" conversation. However, it has so many meanings and uses in informal groups that it is one of the most popular words in spoken English. Still, there are many people who will not use this word, and who will be offended when others use it.

The great English writer Shakespeare wrote, "A rose by any other name would smell as sweet." To follow Shakespeare's example, we might say, "*Excrement*, by any other name would smell as *bad*." But the odor may seem far away or close, depending on what we name it.

Discussion

1. What is the common word for waste material (feces) in your language? Is this an acceptable term, or is it taboo?

2. In your language, write as many synonyms for the word as you know. Can you group the words into social classes? Are these classes the same as the English ones?

3. What is the difference in "attitude" between cow pancakes and cow dung?

4. Why can one word for a body part be "dangerous" and another word for the same body part be "safe?"

5. Why is a certain word not acceptable in a classroom, but widely used in a locker room?

Common Words with Dangerous Double Meanings

Uh-oh! Here's trouble for you: Many ordinary English words have more than one meaning. Most teachers and most textbooks will not warn you about the slang or vulgar meanings of those innocent-sounding words hiding in your vocabulary. Also, although these dangerous meanings are well known to Americans, your bilingual dictionaries will probably not translate meanings into your language.

As a result, you may never know when you are saying something that could have a vulgar meaning. People may laugh, and never tell you why!

For example, the word *ball* has several general meanings.

> **ball** 1. noun. A round rubber toy. "The child is playing with a *ball*." 2. Any sphere. "The sun is a *ball* of fire." 3. A rounded part of the body: the *ball* of the foot 4. A game. "Let's play *ball*." 5. A social party where people dress formally and dance to the music of an orchestra. "The president and his wife attended a *ball* at the Ritz Hotel." 6. In the game of baseball, a pitch that is too high, too low, or not directly over the home plate. "*Ball* four!" shouted the umpire.

Ball is found in common idioms.

7. **Have a ball**: A lot of fun; a very good time. "I had a *ball* at the party last night."

8. **On the ball**: Ready, prepared, smart. "The new assistant seems to be on the *ball*."

Traditional English textbooks and ESL classes won't help you to learn the sexual meanings of *ball*, even though every American adult knows them. If you hear the words used in informal situations, you may not be aware that they are not suited for either formal or polite society.

9. noun. vulgar. Testicle. "He scratched his *balls*.

10. verb. vulgar. To have sexual intercourse with. "Jack and Jill *balled* all night."

There are some very common vulgar expressions that contain the word *ball*.

to have balls verb phrase. vulgar. To have great masculine courage. "Vivian certainly *has balls* to argue with the boss."

it takes balls verb phrase. vulgar. A job or act that requires a person to have great courage. "*It takes balls* to be a race car driver."

to have someone by the balls verb phrase. vulgar. To be in a position capable of hurting someone (as though you were holding his testicles). This may be emotionally, financially, or legally. "The mechanic *had me by the balls*–either I agree to pay his high prices, or I have to get my car towed to a less expensive garage."

to bust one's balls verb phrase. vulgar. To work very hard to complete a difficult job or to attain a goal. "James really *busted his balls* to finish the report on time."

to bust someone's balls verb phrase. vulgar. 1. To make a man lose power or self-esteem as a male. "Maureen enjoys *busting men's balls*. She has a special way of making a man feel inadequate and foolish." 2. To tease, man-to-man. "The guys were *busting my balls* about my getting a promotion."

ball buster noun. vulgar. 1. A difficult test or job. "Professor Jackson's test was a real *ball buster*; nobody was able to answer all the questions." 2. A woman who makes a man feel unmasculine. "Don't try to get friendly with Tara; she's a real *ball buster*. You'll feel like a three-year-old child after a short conversation with her."

oh, balls! vulgar. An expression of disappointment or annoyance. "*Oh, balls!* I can't find my new gloves."

ballsy slang. Courageous; bold. "That was *ballsy* to march up to the professor and ask for a better grade."

How Safe Is Your English? Test Yourself

The following ten words are very common. You probably know their main meaning. But they are dangerous words. They have double meanings. Do you know the *vulgar* meanings of these words? Write the letter of your answer next to the word. Then check your answers on the next page.

1. bang ______	A. homosexual
2. bone ______	B. have oral-genital sex
3. drawers ______	C. have sexual intercourse
4. eat ______	D. underpants
5. fairy ______	E. penis
6. number one ______	F. vagina
7. can ______	G. feces
8. come ______	H. have an orgasm
9. stool ______	I. urine
10. box ______	J. buttocks

Answers

1. C	3. D	5. A	7. J	9. G
2. E	4. B	6. I	8. H	10. F

How many did you get right? ________

1. **bang** (bæŋ) 1. noun. gen. use. A loud noise, like the sound of a gun. "The door closed with a *bang*." 2. noun. Hair cut so that it is combed forward and cut straight over the eyebrows. 3. noun. A thrill or special pleasure. "I get a *bang* out of watching little kids play baseball." 4. verb. To hit and hurt. "He *banged* his head on the door." 5. verb. To hit, making a loud noise. "Someone is *banging* on the door." 6. vulgar. Have sexual intercourse with. Usually the subject is male, the object female. "'I'd really like to *bang* her,' he said to his friend."

2. **bone** (boun) 1. noun. gen. use. Part of a skeleton. "Your body has 206 *bones*." "The dog ate a bone." 2. verb. gen. use. To take the *bones* out of something. "The butcher will *bone* the fish for you." 3. verb. slang. Bone up. To study for a test. "I can't go to the movies with you; I have to *bone* up for the history exam tomorrow." 4. noun. vulgar. The penis, especially when it is erect.

3. **drawers** (drɔːrz) 1. noun, plural. gen. use. Parts of a desk, dresser, or other furniture. "His desk has three *drawers*." 2. noun, plural. gen. use. Underpants. "The new department store is having a sale. I think I'll buy some new *drawers*."

4. **eat** (iːt) 1. verb. gen. use. Chew and swallow food. "We *eat* three meals a day." 2. verb. vulgar. Perform cunnilingus or fellatio. (Lick a partner's genitals.)

5. **fairy** ('fɛə ri) 1. noun. gen. use. A very small imaginary, magical person, usually with wings. "The children love stories about *fairies*." "Cinderella has a *fairy* godmother." 2. noun. slang. A male homosexual. (offensive)

6. **number one** (nʌm bər 'wʌn) 1. adj. gen. use. The best, the most important. "Mr. Hiro is the *number one* man in that company." 2. noun. children's euphemism. Urine. "I have to make *number one*." (= urinate)

7. **can** (cæn) 1. noun. gen. use. A round metal container. Mother opened a *can* of tuna fish. 2. verb. gen. use. Be able. "John *can* speak four languages." 3. verb. gen. use. To put something into cans or jars, such as food. "Rose *canned* four quarts of tomatoes from her garden." 4. noun. slang. The bathroom. The toilet. "Where's Joe?" "He's in the *can*." 5. noun. slang. The buttocks. "I don't like to wear tight slacks because I have a big *can*."

8. **come** (cʌm) 1. verb. gen. use. Move toward the person who is speaking. "*Come* here." 2. verb. gen. use. Arrive. "What time will you *come* to my house?" 2. To be packed in a certain kind of container. "Juice *comes* in pints and quarts." 3. To be available in a certain size, color or style. "This blouse *comes* in red, green and brown." 4. verb. vulgar. Ejaculate. Have an orgasm. "'Did you *come*?' he asked."

9. **stool** (stu:l) 1. noun. gen. use. A chair without a back or arms. "The customers sat on the bar *stools*." 2. noun. formal. medical. Feces; a bowel movement. "The doctor asked the patient to bring in a sample of his *stool*."

10. **box** (bɑks) 1. noun. gen. use. A container; something you can put things in. "The child put his toys into a *box*." 2. verb. gen. use. To put into a box. "The clerk *boxed* and wrapped the gift." 3. verb. gen. use. To fight with one's fists, as in the sport of *boxing*. 4. noun. vulgar. A woman's vagina.

More Dangerous Doubles

Here are eighty-five more common words with dangerous double meanings. You will find the slang or vulgar meanings in the Definitions section of this book starting on page 109.

adult
affair
bag
basket
beat
beaver
bed
behind
blow
bottom
boxers
briefs
buns
brush
bush
can
cheap
cheat
cherry
clap
climax
pet
Peter
piece
piles
privates
put out
queer
relations
come
crabs
crack
cream
Dick
dirty
do
drag
finger
fly
friend
fruit
gas
gay
go
go down
hammer
hard
head
hole
hot
rocks
rubber
runs
safety
satisfy
screw
sixty nine
hump
hung
John
joint
jugs
knob
knocker
lay
loose
lungs
madame
make
meat
member
moon
neck
number two
nuts
organ
overcoat
period
swing
tail
thing
tool
trick
turn on
withdraw

People often tell jokes using words with double meanings. They get a good laugh from others. If you accidentally use these words where they can have a double meaning, people may laugh and you won't know why.

"Do you have red balls?"

For example:
"Do you have red balls?" "He's our number two man." "Put the tool in my box." "Do you want a cherry?" "I like Dick." "Are you hot?" "Would you like a piece?" "I played on my friend's organ." "I need a large tool." "I like to start off each day with a bang."

Discussion

1. Are there common words in your language that have dangerous double meanings?

2. What is the reaction when new speakers of your language use these words?

Religious Taboos

According to the Jewish and Christian religions, God gave His people the Ten Commandments to live by. The third commandment is "You may not misuse the name of God." A religious person *may* say "God" and "Jesus" with respect. He or she may *not* use these names for showing anger, strong emotion, or cursing another person. It is *blasphemy* to do this.

Christ!	For Christ's sake!
Christ almighty!	
Jesus!	Jesus Christ!
God!	God damn it!
Hell! Go to hell!	What the hell!

Many people try not to use these words in formal situations such as school or office, in front of children, or in the company of people they don't know well.

However, you will probably hear these words very often. They are extremely common in expressions of surprise and anger.

Because these words are taboo, some people use a softer way of swearing–at least in formal or mixed company. They say other words that begin with the same sounds:

Cripes!	Christmas!
For crying out loud!	
Gee Whiz!	Jiminy Cricket!
Jeepers!	Cheese and crackers!
Golly!	Goldarnit!
Gosh!	Doggone it!
Heck! Go to heck!	What the heck!

Oh my God! Jesus! and *Jesus Christ!* are commonly said during sexual excitement or orgasm.

How double meanings cause changes in the language.

When a term becomes widely known in its *taboo* meaning, people will stop using the word for its *original* meaning. For example, many years ago, the word *cock* meant a male chicken. This word became a slang word for penis. *Cock* became so widely known as penis that people stopped using the word to mean a male chicken. A new word had to be found for male chicken. A male chicken is now called a rooster.

From 1300 to the 1900s, the word *ass* meant "a small, horse–like animal with long ears." It was an insult to call a person an ass. It meant he or she was as stupid as this animal. But this was not a vulgar term.

A different word, *arse*, was the common vulgar term for buttocks. The word *arse* went through pronunciation changes in some places in England until it had the same sound and spelling as *ass*. The word *ass* now has two meanings.

One meaning is polite, and one is vulgar. The vulgar term "has driven out" the use of the word *ass* to mean an animal. Now all use of the word *ass* seems vulgar. Even the Christian Bible has changed. For Matthew 21:5, an older translation reads, "Behold, your king is coming to you, humble, and mounted on an ass." A newer translation reads: "See, your king comes to you, gentle and riding on a donkey..."

The common word for cat was *pussy* fifty years ago. The word *pussy* became a vulgar word for vagina. Now almost no young person calls a cat a pussy anymore. But the dictionary still defines "pussy" as a cat.

The word *organ* can mean 1. any part of a body, or 2. a musical instrument commonly played in churches. But since the euphemism for penis is "sex organ," the word *organ* is getting to be dangerous. Here is an organ joke–"Did you hear what happened in church last week? Mrs. Jones chased the minister around the church. Finally she caught him by the organ."

Discussion

1. Give examples of words that were in common use but were "driven out" by a taboo double meaning.

2. Has this happened in your language?

3. In your home culture, are there religious words that are taboo?

4. What is the penalty or public reaction if they are said?

5. Are there "safe" alternate pronunciations of these words?

6. When people get hurt or angry, what type of words do they tend to say?

Safe Words for Dangerous Clothing:
Our Underwear

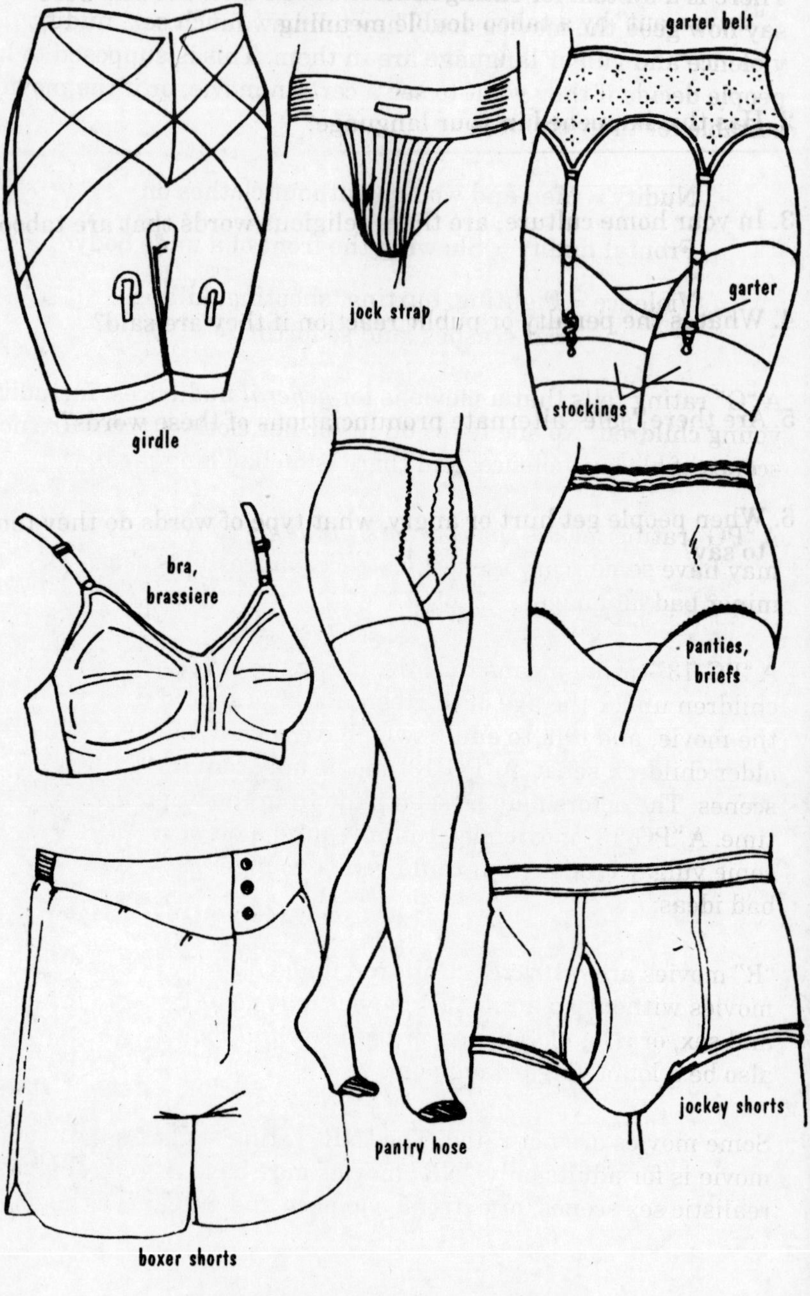

Dangerous English Goes to the Movies

There is a system for rating American movies. The ratings do not say how good the movies are. They tell how much sex, nudity, violence and vulgar language are in them. This is supposed to help people decide if they want to see a certain movie, or if the movie is suitable for their children.

Nudity = Men and women without clothes on

Frontal nudity = Showing the front of a nude body

Violence = Fighting, hurting, shooting, killing, car crashes, and so forth

A "G" rating tells that a movie is for *general* audiences, including young children. No one takes off his or her clothes; there are no scenes of bloody violence; and there is no bad language.

A "PG" rating means that *parents' guidance* is needed. The movie may have some scary scenes, violence, suggestions of sex, or some minor bad language.

A "PG-13" rating means that the movie is *not* recommended for children under the age of thirteen. Parents should read a review of the movie, and talk to adults who have seen it, before letting their older children see it. A "PG-13" movie may contain short sex scenes. The actors may be seen nude from the waist up for a brief time. A "PG-13" movie may contain quite a bit of violence and some vulgar language. It could give a younger child bad dreams or bad ideas.

"R" movies are *restricted.* Children under 17 may not go to these movies without an adult. "R" movies may contain a lot of nudity and sex, or a lot of violence, or both sex *and* violence. There may also be a lot of vulgar language.

Some movies are not rated. The "NR" rating suggests that the movie is for adults only. "NR" movies may have a great deal of realistic sex scenes, or extreme violence and vulgar language.

"X-rated" movies (or videos) usually do not have much story at all. They are *pornographic*. That means they were made for the purpose of sexual excitement. There are many long scenes of sex acts.

Do you have children? Do you have a TV? There are many useful, educational, and entertaining programs on TV. But there also are too many programs that waste time and fill young minds with violence and sexual excitement. In the U.S., parents must be very careful about what their children watch on TV.

There is a rating system for TV programs, too. It is meant to help parents decide what their children watch on TV. Most of the major networks use this system. (There are many cable programs that do not rate their shows yet.)

Y = Suitable for children of all ages
Y-7 = Suitable for children seven years old and older
TV-G = Suitable for all audiences
TV-PG = Parents should guide their children (program may not be suitable)
TV-14 = May not be suitable for children under fourteen
TV-M = For mature audiences only (not suitable for children under eighteen)

In addition, these letters will let you know what is in the program:

V = *Violence*
S = *Sex*
L = Vulgar *language*
D = *Dialogue* (conversation) suggesting sex or violence

The rating will be shown in the upper corner of the screen at the beginning of the show. You can also see it in some of the TV program guides. This rating system became effective late in 1997. It is expected to change from time to time, to respond to the needs of both parents and children.

If you buy a new TV set in the U.S., it will have a "V" chip. This acts like a mini-computer. With the "V" chip, you can program your TV set so it will not show the kinds of programs you do not want your children to watch.

Your Body Talks. Is It Speaking Dangerously?

People speak with their hands and with their whole bodies, as well as with language. But body language is different from one culture to another. A new speaker of English needs to know the nonverbal forms of communication.

Personal space

Adult human beings don't like people to come closer than a certain distance, unless they are "intimates," that is, family members or very close friends or a lover. This unconscious personal distance differs from place to place throughout the world.

An American usually stands about thirty inches (arms length) from the person he or she is talking to. This is the "comfort zone" for conversation. If you come closer, the American may step back, to keep a "comfortable" distance between you. The need for this personal space is part of our culture–but it is not necessarily part of our conscious thinking.

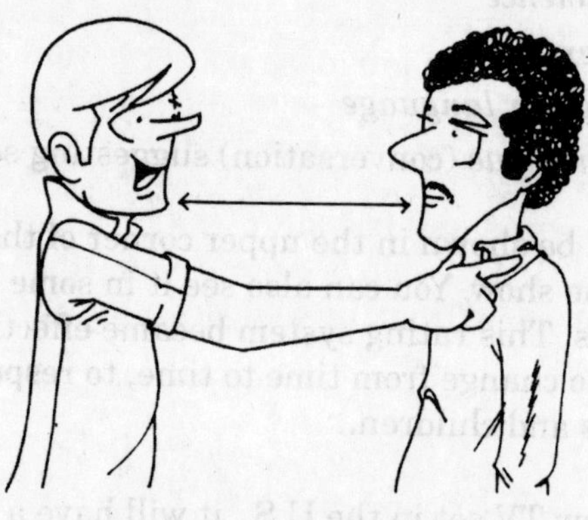

Are you from a culture in which people stand very close when they are talking to each other? Then you may feel that the American is rude for moving away. The American may feel that you are getting "too personal and intimate" if you move in close.

When a man moves closer than arms length, a woman may think that he is sexually interested in her. She may automatically step back if she is not interested, or at least does not want to show that she is. She will feel uncomfortable if she seems "trapped" against a wall or other barrier. Try to stand at a "safe" distance so that the person you are talking to does not get a wrong idea about your intentions.

Are you from a culture where people have a wider "personal space"? Then you may prefer to stand farther away from people you are talking to than an American would. An American will step close to you. This is to stay at his or her most comfortable distance. When you step backward, the American may think that you are cold, distant, or unfriendly. If the American steps toward you again, you may think he or she is too aggressive–perhaps even making a sexual advance. Both of you may very well be mistaken.

Watch how you touch

Touch also has different meanings in different ethnic groups and cultures. Even Americans misinterpret each other. That's because there are so many different American regional, ethnic, age, gender, and personal behaviors.

Observe the touching behavior that goes on around you. Learn to "listen to" this nonverbal language. Observe your own use of touch among different members of family and friends. It is quite fascinating.

Are Americans warm and friendly? Or are they cool and unfriendly? Your impression of Americans will be based on the culture that *you* come from, as well as on the American individuals you meet.

Greetings

Men shake hands when they are introduced to other men. Men generally shake hands with male friends to say hello, and may also give a firm pat on the shoulder, or a slap on the upper back.

In business, women offer their hand when they are introduced to others. In social situations, a woman shakes hands sometimes, but sometimes she doesn't. It is OK either way. If a woman offers her hand, shake hands.

A firm handshake is considered a sign of good character and self-confidence. A weak handshake is considered a sign of a weak, ineffective, or very gentle person. "That person shakes hands like a dead fish," someone might say of a person whose hand is limp. Ask Americans to show you the proper handshake grip if you are in doubt.

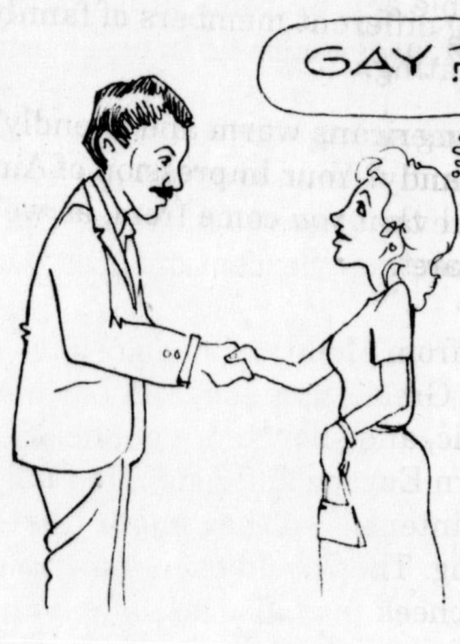

Hugging

Many American women hug close friends when greeting them, especially if it has been a long time since they last saw them. A woman may hug a friend (male or female) to congratulate him or her on a birthday, a graduation, or good news. Friends may hug to give or receive thanks for a gift or a favor. Or they may hug to show sympathy for someone's loss, or a disappointment. The hugs between men and women *or* between women and women may be accompanied by a light kiss. This may be on the cheek or be a brief "smack" on the lips, or even just in the air between the two pairs of lips! Usually, there are no sexual intentions in these hugs. Do not mistake either a hug or a quick kiss from a friend as an invitation to romance or sex.

Men may hug women when they see them after a long absence. They might hug to offer congratulations, to thank them for a gift, or to cheer them up when they are sad.

Hugging is becoming more common among men. In the past, most American men did not hug other men, except family members. To show friendship or sympathy, they clapped a hand on the shoulder. Today, many men hug their men friends, but most do not. Hugging among athletes upon victory and celebration is the rule. A slap on the buttocks after a good athletic feat is also (usually) both acceptable and welcome. It is not then a sign of homosexual behavior, as it might be in other settings.

If you hug someone, don't hold on too long. Observe the behaviors of men and women around you. There are great ethnic and personal variations to hugging. The following are generalizations. (There are many exceptions.)

People from Mediterranean origins (Italian, French, Jewish, Arabic, Greek, Spanish, and Latin American) generally touch more in public, and show more public affection, than do people from northern Europe and Asia. Men may hug other men with no sexual intent. And they might use their hands a lot when speaking. They could even touch you while talking to you. Kisses on the cheek may also be common to them when greeting friends.

If you are on the West Coast (in California), you can expect to see more people hugging each other than on the East Coast. People may hug each other hello and goodbye, even on a first meeting, if they are introduced by a good mutual friend, or have some strong common interest.

At one time, teachers in elementary school frequently hugged the younger students. In many states, hugging children is now against school rules. That is because of a few very highly publicized cases of teachers who were *pedophiles* (people attracted sexually to children). They became teachers in order to get sexual contact with children. There have been other cases of students who accused teachers of touching them in a wrong way, but these students were angry about failing grades. They wanted to get the teachers in trouble. To protect the schools from lawsuits, rules were made against hugging children.

People of Asian backgrounds, or Northern European backgrounds (German, English, Norwegian, Swedish, etc.) generally are more "reserved." They generally show less affection in public.

There are books and articles about the benefits of hugging. These articles encourage people to hug their friends and family members. One American psychologist wrote: "Four hugs a day is the minimum daily requirement. Eight is better. Twelve hugs a day will make sure we stay in the best of health."

Public kissing by two young people who either are "in love" or are strongly attracted to each other is quite common in cities, on beaches, and at young people's parties. A couple may walk down the street holding hands, or have their arms around each other. One can now also see homosexual couples holding hands, hugging, and kissing. Many mature people think that "necking" (passionate kissing) in public shows very bad manners, however.

A woman may hold hands with, or walk with an arm around, another woman if she is a sister, relative, or very close friend. In America, if men kiss, or walk holding hands, most others will assume that they have a homosexual relationship.

The movement for gay people's rights in the United States has increased public acceptance of gay and lesbian life styles. As a result, more gay people are frank and open about their sexual orientation. But, in many places there is still "gay-bashing." This strong prejudice against gay people includes name-calling, job and housing discrimination, and even physical attacks by homophobic thugs (uneducated men who fear homosexuality). This danger causes some gay people to continue to hide their sexual identification from most other people.

In the gay community, hugging is more common. A person new to a closed group may be hugged on departure, if the overall feeling is that he or she is accepted into the group.

We talk with our hands, but what are we saying?

Our hands help us to communicate without speaking. However, the meanings of nonverbal gestures are not the same around the world. A polite gesture in your culture may be a vulgar gesture in the U.S. The following are some common American hand gestures.

"The nose salute" is a strong insult, that is practiced especially among angry children. Sometimes the person also sticks out his or her tongue while wiggling the four "nose" fingers. Translation: I hate you; I'm angry; I think you stink. Among adults, the translation might be "Kiss my ass."

The most common vulgar gesture is "giving the finger." The translation of this is "Up your ass," "Up yours" or "Sit on this." It's used to show contempt, anger, or hatred. The middle finger is extended, and the other fingers are folded. The hand is waved upward at the other person, with the back of the hand facing the observer.

(Do not use your middle finger to point with, or to count "one" with. It will look as though you are "giving someone the finger.")

A gesture that came into English through Italian body language is the "Italian salute." A person places the left hand on the lower part of the upper right arm. The right arm is brought quickly upwards and backwards, folding over the left hand. The translation is "Fuck you."

Another "Fuck you" gesture is made by holding the tip of the thumb on the inside of the front teeth (mouth open, of course) and then flicking it out.

A gesture of approval of a woman's sexiness is this: The fingers of one hand are brought up to the lips, which are pursed as if blowing smoke or whistling. The person may close his eyes and kiss his fingers, then open his hand toward the object he admires. (This might also be done in appreciation of a delicious meal.)

Men's-room behavior

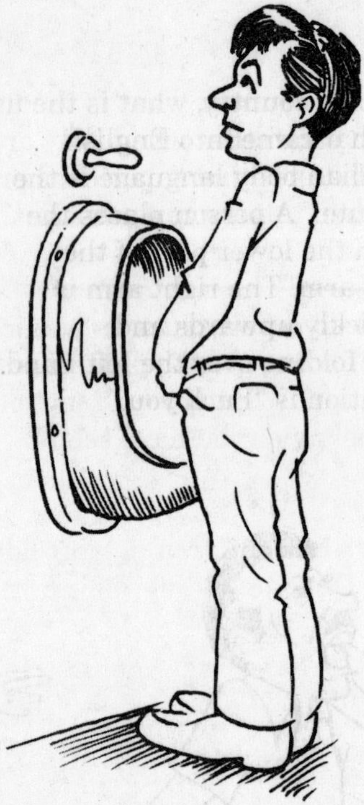

In a men's room that has many urinals, American men almost never stand next to someone else unless all the other units are in use. A man is expected to look up or look down, or straight ahead, but not to the left or right. To look at another man can be dangerous, and may be taken as an offer of sex.

Little boys–up to the age of six or so–usually go into the ladies' room with their mothers if there is no male to take them into the men's room.

Discussion:

1. In your home country, what is the usual distance that people stand from each other when they are talking? Is it very different from the distance that Americans prefer? How does this make you feel when talking to Americans?

2. How much do people touch in public in your home country? Hug? Kiss? What are the differences between men and women in this regard? What is your reaction to the American public touching behavior you have seen?

3. Do teachers hug children in your home country? If they do, up to what age? Do parents hug their own children? Up to what age?

4. What is your reaction, "Twelve hugs a day lead to the best of health?"

5. Are there any American gestures that have different meanings in your culture? Have any of your gestures been misunderstood by Americans?

Sexual Harassment: What's that?

Sexual harassment is unwelcome attention or sexual behavior that comes from others at school, at work or at any other place that one is not free to just walk away from.

Sexual harassment might mean using vulgar language, telling "dirty" jokes, or making comments about a person's body or sexiness. It might be unwelcome touching, invitations to date, or talking about one's sexual abilities. It could be hanging up pictures or calendars with women or men in bathing suits (or nude). What was OK a few years ago, or is now OK in your home culture, may not be suitable behavior in today's American business office.

Supervisors of employees have a lot of power over the workers–they can fire them, transfer them, and control their performance reviews, pay raises, and so forth. When a supervisor makes an unwanted comment, invitation, or sexual request, an employee who does not wish to respond may fear losing his or her job.

New laws say that employers or supervisors may not use their position of power to sexually harass their employees. Schools and business companies have been sued for allowing sexual harassment to occur.

The new rules and laws are to protect each group against sexual harassment by the other. Both men and women must be careful of what they say and do to members of the opposite sex, especially at work or school, but also in many other circumstances. If an employer or supervisor offends you at work, ask him or her politely to stop, or report the behavior to *their* supervisor. Some work places have committees for handling difficult employee relations.

Can people fall in love at work? Of course. But the workplace is considered a dangerous place in which to look for a social life. Most romances end before long. If there are bad personal feelings at work, one doesn't want to leave a job, too.

In schools and universities, there have always been strict rules that say a teacher is not allowed to date, or have a romantic relationship with, a student. In the military, an officer may be court-martialed for "fraternizing" (dating, and/or having a sexual relationship) with a person of lower rank. The punishment can be severe: years in jail, and a dishonorable discharge.

Discussion

1. What are the rules regarding sexual harassment in the place where you work or attend classes?

2. Are men and women protected from sexual harassment in your home country? How?

3. Is there any behavior between men and women that is acceptable in the United States that is *not* acceptable in your home country?

Who Are All These People?

It's important to know the acceptable, polite terms for ethnic groups and races.

The United States is a land of many different races and nationalities. Native Americans, African Americans, Europeans, Middle Easterners, and Asians live and get along remarkably well together here.

Americans are of many different religions, too. In the U.S. there are more than one hundred denominations (groups, types) of Christians, and four of Jews, plus many congregations of Mormons, Muslims, Buddhists, Hindus, and Unitarians. There are also some Americans who believe in many gods and many Americans who believe in no god.

In the U.S. there are all sorts of friendships, business partnerships, and marriages involving people from different national backgrounds or religions. Many Americans are "mixtures" or "blends" of two, four, or eight different ethnic groups. Americans are proud of having more than one culture, language, or ethnic group in their family history. The English language, the love of being unique, and the appreciation of our rights and freedoms combine to hold us all together.

A distinctly American ideal is that *all people must be treated equally*. Americans are taught both in church and school to respect others. National U.S. laws say that we may not discriminate based on race, color, religion, gender, or national origin. *All* people must have a fair chance to get an education, to find a place to live, to get a job. There are even special laws against "hate crimes" that hurt people because of race or nationality. We must live in peace *together*. That means all of us. The law says so.

But these ideals are not yet completely real. There is unfairness in employment and housing. There are tensions and misunderstandings among the races and between different national groups. There still is prejudice in some people's hearts. Thoughtful people must continue to work toward making the ideal real.

One sign of the tension is the names that people call other groups. Some of these labels are meant to be humorous. Others are insults. The words have a history of being said with anger, or discrimination. Since many of these terms are extremely offensive, someone hearing them may get angry enough even to fight.

The newcomer or foreign visitor in the United States should learn the correct names of each national and racial group. If you use derogatory names, people may think that you are a bigot (a person who holds prejudices, and treats others unfairly). You could get into very bad trouble!

Even for Americans, it isn't easy to know which names are OK. A name for a certain group may be an insult in California, but acceptable on the East Coast. The correct names for groups of people can, in fact, change. Also, older people in a group may use a name for themselves, but one that younger people take as an insult. Similarly, a member of a group may use a derogatory name for his own group, but may get angry if someone else uses that word.

Within just a few years after this book is published, some of the names that we include as "acceptable" may change. Hopefully, one day people will say, "There is only one race, and that's the human race. We are all citizens of one planet." If so, maybe people can stop worrying about "names" of all sorts.

Warning: In the following list of names that people have called others, you will find some of the most dangerous and offensive words in all of the English language.

First, what might you, the readers of this book be called?

alien ('ei li: ən) noun. (Once acceptable, this word is beginning to sound offensive in some contexts.) A person who is living in or visiting a country of which he or she is not a citizen. The word is also used to refer to a science fiction creature from outer space.

foreign adjective. From another country. OK in the expression *foreign country*, and in *foreign-born*, but on college campuses, it is no longer politically correct in the term *foreign student*.

foreigner noun. (Once completely acceptable, this word is beginning to sound offensive to some people.) A person who was born outside the U.S. and has not become a citizen. *Foreign-born person* is more widely accepted.

foreign student This term was acceptable and widely used up to the 1980s. It then came to be considered offensive by college administrators: "It made students from other countries seem not to belong here." The term was changed to *international student*, showing that people from around the world were contributing a positive presence to the colleges. However, the government still uses the term *foreign student*. The words *foreign service*, *foreign currency*, and *foreign diplomat* are still used. To give an immediate example of how authors and others incorporate language changes such as this: the first edition of this book (1980) was named *A Foreign Student's Guide to Dangerous English*. The title of the second edition (1990) was changed to *An Indispensable Guide to Dangerous English for Language Learners and Others*.

illegal alien Acceptable until recently, this term is considered by some people to be extremely offensive. Still used by the government and in laws, this is being replaced in polite conversation among educated people by *unlawful resident*, *undocumented immigrant*, or *person who is living in the United States unlawfully*.

immigrant (acceptable) noun. A person who comes to work and live in a new country, and gives up his or her allegiance to a former country.

international student (acceptable) A student from another country who attends a U.S. college.

tourist (acceptable) noun. A person who is traveling for pleasure.

visitor (acceptable) noun. A person who is in the United States temporarily, including tourists and temporary workers.

That's who *you* are. Now to find out who everyone else is. Each group below is listed under the most common, acceptable term. All the other terms for that group are indented and listed alphabetically.

African (acceptable) A person born in Africa, and particularly a black African. It is, however, preferable to use the exact nationality if you know it: Congolese, Nigerian, Somalian, Ghanaian, Sudanese, Rwandan, and so forth. People from Egypt, Morocco, Tunisia, Algeria, and Libya are thought more of as North Africans or Arabic rather than Africans although they too are from the continent of Africa.

African American (acceptable) An American citizen whose ancestors came from Africa. The politically correct name has changed several times in the past forty years. The history of slavery left a great many scars on society in the U.S. The road to full equality for African Americans has been slow, and sometimes violent. In the struggle for full civil rights, many of their leaders proposed new names for themselves.

black also, Black (acceptable) This was the preferred term from 1960s to 1990. It came in with the slogan "Black Is Beautiful." Before that, the term was considered offensive. It had been related to insults and other negative uses of the word *black*.

blood (slang) This term is used by African Americans to refer to other African Americans. It is a short word meaning *blood brother*.

boy (derogatory) This term is extremely offensive when used by a white person speaking to an adult African American. It implies that the black person is not a full adult equal to the speaker.

brother (slang) Short for *blood brother* and *soul brother*. Used by African-Americans for each other. Shortened to "bro."

colored adjective. **colored person** noun. These were the acceptable terms until the 1960s, at least in many southern states. They still are used by many older people who have not been listening to the news. Today these words sound uneducated, and may be considered offensive.

Negro ('ni: grou) This was an acceptable term from the 1920s to the early 1960s. It is still widely used by older people. Younger people use the word Negro as a derogatory term; they mean a black person who does not support black political causes.

nigger (vulgar; extremely offensive when used by a non-black person) Originally, this word was a slurred pronunciation of Negro. It has an ugly history. It was used in connection with slavery, murders, prejudice, rape, hatred, house burnings, and all forms of discrimination against African Americans. This makes it the most hated word in our language. This word, spoken by a white person, will remind others of the ugliness of racism. The word can cause extreme anger. Educated non-black people avoid this hurtful word above all other words. (Many educated people also avoid the people who use "the N-word.")

On the other hand, an African American may freely use this word with another person as a term of friendship, often pronouncing it **niggah**: "Yo *Niggah*, what up?" Non-black friends and associates may also use the term *but only when completely welcomed and integrated into black social circles*. The word *nigger* may be used by blacks to mean *person*: "Who's that *nigger* over there?"

field nigger (vulgar) and **field slave** (These terms are used by some black activists to describe themselves.) A black person who does not love, or want to be like, white people.

house nigger (vulgar; offensive) and **house slave** (These terms are used by blacks to refer to certain other black persons.) A black person who takes the white society's point of view.

(In the times of slavery, African slaves who worked in the master's house were generally treated better than the slaves who worked in the fields. The house slaves identified with, and in many cases, loved, their masters. The slaves who worked in the fields were generally poorly treated, and hated the master.)

Oreo cookie; **Oreo** ('ɔːr iː ou) (offensive) A black person who has many or all of the manners and behavior and ways of thinking that a white person has. (An Oreo cookie is a "sandwich" of two chocolate cookies with a white filling between them.) The nickname hints that the person referred to is "black on the outside, white on the inside."

people of color (acceptable) This is a rather recent term that has been introduced by political activists. It includes all non-white people (African, Native American, Latino, and Asian). It is used both for "third world" and "oppressed" people–which is to say people from poor, non-industrialized countries, and poor people living within industrialized countries.

pickaninny (offensive) A black child.

Uncle Tom (offensive) This is a negative term that African Americans may use for a black person who seems to take sides with white people and reject people of his or her own race.

These terms for black people are very offensive: **boogie**, **coon**, **jigaboo**, **jungle bunny**, **sambo**, **shade**, **spade**, **spook**.

American (acceptable) People in the United States call themselves *Americans*. There is no other simple word for the nationality. Of course, people in Central and South America also are Americans. There, they call people from the United States *North Americans*. But that term includes Canadians and Mexicans, too.

Anglo (acceptable) noun, adjective. A white English-speaking American. This term is a derogatory word used by Mexican Americans. But Americans do not find it offensive. Today it is accepted by the U.S. and state governments, newspapers, and educators to refer to native English-speakers.

Gringo (Mexican and Southwestern use: derogatory) noun. Any non-Mexican, but especially an American. The term is often intended as an insult, but is usually accepted with good humor by Americans. Americans may also call themselves "Gringo" when they are with their Spanish-speaking Mexican friends.

U.S. citizen (acceptable)

Yankee This name is acceptable to *most* Americans, who proudly use the nickname to mean themselves. However, in the South, "Yankee" means "Northerner," and thus, it is used as an insult. Now and then people in some other countries use this name in anger, saying "Yankee go home!"

Arab ('æ rəb) (acceptable) A person from any Arabic-speaking country such as Saudi Arabia. It is preferable to use the exact nationality if it is known: Algerian, Egyptian, Iraqi, Jordanian, Libyan, Moroccan, Palestinian, Saudi or Saudi Arabian, Syrian, Tunisian, Yemeni.

Ayrab ('ei ræb) (derogatory) An Arab.

Asian ('ei ʒən) (acceptable) *Formal*: A person from the continent of Asia. *Informal*: A person from Eastern Asia: Chinese, Korean or Japanese. It is better to use the specific nationality, if known: Afghan, Bengal, Cambodian, Chinese, Filipino, Indian, Japanese, South Korean, North Korean, Laotian, Malaysian, Nepalese, Pakistani, Thai, Tibetan, Vietnamese.

Oriental noun, adjective. A person from the Orient (the Far East). The word is no longer "politically correct." Some people have found it offensive because it defines others by their geographic relationship to the Europe or the United States. If you use this term, educated people will know you are "out of date." As an adjective in terms such as *oriental rug*, it is still acceptable.

When you don't know the specific nationality, use *Asian*. It shows thoughtlessness to call a person Chinese or Japanese when in fact he or she is not.

The following terms for Asians are all very offensive: **gook**, **slant**, **dink**, **slope**, **zip**.

British (acceptable) The people of Great Britain, and particularly of England.

Brit (acceptable in informal speech.)

English (acceptable) People from England. (The term does not include the Scots and the Welsh.)

Limey ('laɪ mi) (humorous, sometimes derogatory.) This nickname came from British sailors' custom of eating limes. This kept them healthy when they were at sea.

WASP (White Anglo-Saxon Protestant) (slang) "The people in power." Anglo-Saxon refers to people from northern Europe–English, Dutch, German, etc. All of the American presidents have been WASP, except John F. Kennedy, who was an Irish Catholic. The image of the WASP is that of a rich, white, well-educated, powerful type of person who controls companies, banks, stocks, Wall Street, the government, and so on. The term often is meant to be derogatory.

Canadian (acceptable) A person from Canada.

Canuck (kə ˈnʌk) (Acceptable in western Canada, this word is offensive in the northeastern United States.) Canadian or French Canadian.

Chinese (acceptable) A person from mainland China. A person of Chinese descent.

Chinese American (acceptable) An American citizen of Chinese descent.

Taiwanese (acceptable) A person from Taiwan. This term is used by Chinese people from Taiwan to distinguish themselves from Chinese who come from mainland China.

These terms for Chinese are offensive: **Chinaman**, **Chink**, **Chinee**, **chow**, **coolie**, **chopsticks**, **dink**, **fortune cookie**, **slant**, **slope**. The term **banana** is also offensive. It refers to an Asian who acts like a white person or takes a "white" point of view. (Yellow on the outside, white on the inside.)

Cuban (ˈkyu bən) (acceptable) A person from Cuba.

Cuban American (acceptable) An American citizen of Cuban descent.

Cube (kyu:b) (offensive) A person from Cuba.

Czech (tʃɛk) (acceptable) A person from the Czech Republic (part of the former Czechoslovakia).

The term **Bohunk** can be offensive. It refers to a Bohemian–a person from Bohemia, an area in the Czech Republic. It has been also applied to any Czech, Slovak or Hungarian.

Filipino (acceptable) A person from the Philippines.

Flip (sometimes offensive) A Filipino.

French (acceptable) A person from France or of French descent.

frog, frog eater, froggy (humorous or mildly derogatory) A French person.

French Canadian (acceptable) A Canadian citizen of French descent.

German (acceptable) A person from Germany.

German American (acceptable) An American of German descent.

These terms for German are offensive: **Germ**, **Germy**, **Heinie** ('haɪ ni), **Hun**, **Jerry**, **Kraut** (kraʊt).

Hungarian (acceptable) A person from Hungary, or of Hungarian descent.

These terms for Hungarian are offensive: **Hun**, **Hunkie**.

Indian 1. (acceptable) A person from India. 2. (becoming unacceptable) A native American.

IndoChinese (acceptable) A person from Vietnam, Cambodia, Laos, or Thailand. It is preferable to use the exact nationality if you know it: **Vietnamese**, **Cambodian**, **Laotian**, **Hmong**, **Thai**, and so forth.

These terms are extremely offensive: **slant**, **gook**.

Irish (acceptable) A person from Ireland, or of Irish descent.

These terms may be offensive: **Mick**, **Paddy**, **Irisher**.

Italian (acceptable) A person from Italy.

Italian American (acceptable) An American of Italian descent.

Mafiosi Members of an organized crime family or Mafia. (When this term is applied to Italians in general, it is extremely offensive.)

These terms for Italian are also offensive: **Dino**, **Dago**, **greaseball**, **Guinea**, **Eyetalian**, **macaroni**, **spaghetti bender**, **Wop**.

Japanese (acceptable) A person from Japan.

Japanese American (acceptable) An American of Japanese descent.

These terms for Japanese are offensive: **Jap**, **Nip**, **slant**, **slope**, **yap**, **zip**.

Latino (Latina for a woman) (acceptable) noun, adjective. A person of Latin American descent. This name includes Spanish-speaking and Portuguese-speaking people of the United States, and Central and South America. This term is preferred by political activists over the older term, *Hispanic*. It includes more people.

Hispanic (hɪs 'pæ nɪk) (acceptable, but not everywhere) noun, adjective. A Spanish speaker or person of Spanish-speaking descent.

Chicano (tʃɪ 'kɑ nou) (acceptable) noun, adjective. Americans of Mexican descent, particularly in Texas, California, New Mexico, and Arizona. This was once a derogatory word used by English-speakers. It was adopted as the name they preferred, by people of Mexican descent who were born in the United States. The term implies "activist," people who are working for their rights.

Spic (derogatory) noun. A Spanish-speaking person.

Mexican American (acceptable) noun, adjective. American of Mexican descent.

These terms for Mexicans or Mexican Americans are offensive: **Mex, taco, tamale, greaser, bean eater, chili eater**.

wetback noun. A very poor person from Mexico who swam the Rio Grande to come to the United States illegally to work. Also, a person who entered the country unlawfully to work on a farm or to do other menial labor.

bracero noun. A legal, temporary migrant worker from Mexico.

Puerto Rican (acceptable) noun, adjective. A person from Puerto Rico. (Puerto Ricans are American citizens, although Puerto Rico is not a state.)

P.R. (less acceptable) noun. A person from Puerto Rico.

Rican (may be acceptable or offensive, depending on how it is used) A person from Puerto Rico.

Nooyorreecan (ˈnuː yɔːr ˈiː kən) (New York Rican) (Humorous and acceptable in the U.S.) A Puerto Rican living in New York. (Possibly offensive in Puerto Rico.)

Spaniard, Spanish (acceptable) noun, adjective. A person from Spain.

Do not say "Spanish person" when you do *not* mean "a person from Spain." It is better to use the exact nationality if you know it: American, Dominican, Cuban, Mexican, Guatemalan, Costa Rican, Honduran, Nicaraguan, Panamanian, Venezuelan, Colombian, Peruvian, Ecuadoran, Argentine, Chilean, Paraguayan, Uruguayan, or Bolivian; or the term **South American**, **Hispanic**, or **Latino**. Or, **Spanish-speaker**.

Brazilian (acceptable) A person from Brazil.

Portuguese (acceptable) A person from Portugal.

native (acceptable) A person born in a certain place. A **native New Yorker** was born in New York City.

native American (acceptable) This word is used to mean a person born in the United States. But when the N is capitalized, the meaning changes. The term is now ambiguous. **American-born person** is clearer.

Native American (acceptable) noun, adjective. A person descended from any of the native people who lived in America before Europeans arrived.

Indian (less acceptable) noun, adjective. Since Columbus thought he was in the Indies, he mistakenly named the people he met *Indians*. The word *Indian* remains in our language, literature, and popular culture. It refers to people of a very wide variety of ethnic groups, grouping them all together with no distinctions. Descendants of these original Americans refer to themselves by their own tribal names. If you know it, use the right one. Examples: *Cherokee*, *Chippewa*, *Onondaga*, *Dakota*, *Navajo*, *Mohawk*.

Injin (slang, derogatory) noun. A Native American.

Redskin (derogatory) noun. A Native American. Native American groups have asked the major-league baseball teams the Atlanta Braves and the Cleveland Indians and the major league football team, the Washington Redskins to change their names. As of late 1997, this had not happened. Many college teams with names reflecting Native Americans have changed their names, for example, the Montclair Redskins became the Montclair Red Hawks.

squaw (sometimes offensive) noun. Indian woman. This term is also a slang, affectionate/humorous term for one's wife.

apple (offensive) noun. A Native American who is not loyal to his or her race (red on the outside, white on the inside).

Other terms offensive to Native Americans: **Indian giver**, **buck**, **savage**.

Pole (acceptable) A person from Poland. **Polish** (acceptable) adjective.

Polish American (acceptable) An American of Polish descent.

Polack (derogatory)

Romany ('rɑ mə ni) (acceptable) A person descended from the traditionally nomadic people from northern India who now live in various European countries–especially Hungary, the Czech Republic, and Slovakia.

Gypsy (offensive) The name most well known by others for the Romany. The term also means anyone who moves from one home to another frequently without setting down roots in the community.

Roma ('rou mə) (acceptable) the name Romany people sometimes call themselves.

White (acceptable) A person of European or Middle Eastern descent, with light-colored skin, and hair ranging from straight to wavy or curly.

Caucasian (kɔ ˈkei ʒən) (acceptable; formal) A member of the "White" race. This includes, people indigenous to Europe, northern Africa, southwestern Asia, and India.

The following terms are used by African Americans to refer to a white person. They are derogatory: **Charlie**, **Mr. Charlie**, **chicken lips**, **cracker**, **dog**, **gray**, **honky**, **pig**, **silk**, **fay**, **ofay**, **the Man**, **marshmallow**, **white trash**, **vanilla**, **Whitie**, **white boy**, **white girl**.

pale face (derogatory) Used by Native Americans.

cracker (offensive) noun, adjective. White Southerner, not educated.

redneck (derogatory) noun, adjective. An uneducated white person who has many prejudices against other people.

Person of mixed parentage (acceptable) Refers to a person whose parents were of different races: black/white; black/Asian; black/native American; white/Asian; or white/Native American.

biracial (baɪ ˈrei ʃəl) (acceptable) Having parents of two different races.

Creole (acceptable) This term has many different meanings. In the U.S., it is a person of French descent in Louisiana. It is also the language of people of African descent from Haiti.

multiracial (mʌl tɪ ˈrei ʃəl) (acceptable) Of parents of two or more different races.

These words for people having parents of different races are offensive: **half-breed**, **half-caste**, **cross-breed**, **mongrel**.

zebra (offensive) Having one black and one white parent.

Mestizo (mɛs ˈtiː zou) (offensive) Having one Indian and one Spanish parent.

high yaller (yellow) (slang, offensive) A light-skinned African American.

light skin (currently acceptable) A light-skinned person of African descent.

mulatto (mʊ 'lat ou) (offensive; it was acceptable twenty years ago) Of mixed parentage: black and white.

octoroon (ɑk tə 'ruːn) (offensive) Person with one great-grandparent black (hence, one eighth black).

quadroon (kwɑ 'druːn) (offensive) Person with one grandparent black.

Religious names and slurs

Americans remind each other to stay away from conversations about religion, in order not to offend others of different religious beliefs, or get into an argument.

This list contains the acceptable and not acceptable uses of both spoken and written religious terms.

agnostic (æg 'nɑ stɪk) (acceptable) A person who feels that it is not possible to know whether there is a god or not.

atheist ('ei θiː ɪst) (acceptable) A person who believes there is no god.

Buddhist ('buː dɪst)/('bʊ dɪst) (acceptable) A follower of Buddha.

Christian (acceptable) A follower of the teachings of Jesus Christ, and a member of one of the various sects. There are more than one hundred denominations (varieties) of Christians in the United States listed in the *1997 World Almanac*.

Protestant ('prɑ tə stənt) (acceptable) A Christian belonging to one of many different branches of Christianity that began after 1615: **Lutheran**, **Episcopal**, **Presbyterian**, **Methodist**, **Baptist**, **Christian Scientists**, **Jehovah's Witness**, **Latter Day Saints (Mormons)**, **Pentecostal**, **Seventh Day Adventist**, **Reformed Church**, and many more.

Catholic ('kæθ lɪk)/('kæ θə lɪk) (acceptable) A Christian of the older church branch of Christianity, founded by Peter, the chosen first disciple of Jesus Christ.

Bible thumper (derogatory) A person with strong Christian beliefs who tries to convince others of his or her right position by quoting the Bible a lot.

Bible Belter (offensive) The "Bible Belt" is a wide area across the southern and midwestern states. A large percentage of the people in this area are Southern Baptists, with strong fundamental Christian beliefs.

Holy Rollers (hou liː 'rou lərz) (derogatory) Pentecostal Christians who become very energized during religious services, "rolling on the floor" when the Holy Spirit enters them.

Jesus Freak ('dziː zəs friːk) (offensive) A member of a religious sect that encourages new converts to give up all their attachments to family and earthly belongings, and live by begging donations from others.

cult (kʌlt) (derogatory) A system of belief that requires unusual behavior on the part of its members. (Such as leaving families, giving up careers, begging for handouts on the street, collecting guns and armaments for a showdown with the government, preparing for the end of the world, and so forth.)

Judaism ('dzuː diː ɪ zəm) (acceptable)
The religion of the Jews.

Jew (dzuː) (acceptable) noun. A person descended from the early Israelites; a follower of the Jewish religion. The word has both ethnic and religious meanings. **Jewish** adjective.

Hasidim (hæ 'sɪ dɪm) (acceptable) Orthodox Jews who follow religious law very strictly.

These names for Jewish people are offensive: **Bagel bender**, **Hymie**, **Jake**, **Jewboy**, **Hebe**, **Ikey**, **Mocky**, **Shylock**, **Sheeny**, **Yid**.

The term to *Jew down*, meaning to bargain with someone for a lower price is extremely offensive.

Jewish American Princess, often abbreviated **JAP** (offensive). A Jewish girl or woman who thinks she is better than others and deserves expensive things.

Gentile ('dzɛn taɪl) (acceptable) noun, adjective. A word used by Jews and others for any person who is not a Jew.

Goy (noun, singular) **Goyim** ('gɔi əm) (noun, plural) This is a mildly offensive term used by Jews for non-Jews. These terms may be used in a derogatory manner: **Shagitz** A male non-Jew; **schikse** (female non-Jew).

Hindu ('hɪn duː) (acceptable) A believer in Hinduism. Hinduism is a religion of northern India, with beliefs in reincarnation and a god of many forms.

dot head (offensive) An Indian woman who wears a red dot on her forehead.

Islam ('ɪs lɑm)/(ɪs 'lɑːm) (acceptable) noun. The religion founded by Mohammed. Also, the region where Islam is practiced. Islamic ('ɪz lɑ mɪc) adjective.

Muslim ('mʌz ləm)/('mʊz ləm) (acceptable) A follower of the religion of Islam.

Moslem ('mɑz ləm) Outdated term, often used as an adjective. The preferred adjective is *Islamic*.

Mohammedan A follower of Mohammed. No longer an acceptable term for *Muslim*.

Black Muslim noun. (acceptable) A term used in the media to describe American blacks who had converted to Islam. Many have changed their Christian names to Islamic names. The most famous of these were well-known sports heroes: Cassius Clay became Mohammed Ali.

Moonies (ˈmuː niːz) (offensive) A member of the Church of Unification, founded by Reverend Sun Myung Moon.

pagan (ˈpei gən) (acceptable) A person who believes in many gods, or in one of the pre-Christian religions. **pagan** (offensive) A person with no religion; a non-Christian, non-Jew, non-Muslim.

heathen (offensive) A person who is not a Christian, Jew or Muslim; an uncivilized or unenlightened person.

Discussion

1. What are the acceptable terms for your racial, ethnic, and religious groups?

2. What causes people to use racial slurs? Have you had any experiences with people who make racial slurs?

3. What does saying a racial slur say about the person making the slur?

4. What racial and ethnic groups live in your home country? Which group is in the majority? Are minorities treated fairly? Are there racial or ethnic tensions? Are there names for ethnic or racial groups that are very offensive and can cause violence?

5. Quick Quiz: What do you call people who are born in the following countries?

   a. China
   b. Japan
   c. Poland
   d. Canada
   e. the United States
   f. Britain
   g. Greece
   h. Italy

6. What is a term that includes all South and Central Americans?

7. What is a term that includes all dark-skinned people?

8. What is a term that includes all Chinese, Vietnamese, Japanese, Koreans, Thai, Cambodians, and Laotians (among others)?

The New Taboo: Politically Incorrect Words

Fairness is an American ideal. But, as in other countries, people in America don't always treat all others fairly. We have already spoken of the unfairness shown to racial, ethnic, and religious minorities. There has also been unfairness to women, people with physical differences, gay people, children, and the elderly. Some unfairness is in the law. Some unfairness is in people's hearts.

Our history is full of change. This change came from groups of activists who organized to work together to change the laws. They worked to have people become more tolerant of those who are different from themselves.

Some groups took new names for themselves. The old name seemed offensive and hurtful. Only a few years ago, people used them without thinking. But the names had "attitudes" along with their meanings. The names identified people by their differences, and set them apart from "normal" people. A considerate person will no longer use these words. Using these words in some contexts can be as dangerous as using vulgar language. In the past ten or fifteen years, hundreds of words have been labeled *politically incorrect*. Speakers and writers are encouraged to use the new, *politically correct*, terms.

For example, children born with a certain genetic disability used to be labeled *Mongoloid idiots*. All of these individuals have had a similar facial appearance, with narrow eyes. Many, but not all, of them have had very low intelligence. Today these individuals are more objectively referred to as people with *Down's syndrome*.

People who could not use their legs, were blind or deaf, or were missing any limbs, were seen to be "handicapped." This word made people think of them as poor, pitiful, unable to do many ordinary things, and unable to work. *Handicapped* and *disabled* are labels that they have come to hate. However, these words are still in common use by the government.

The names taken on by groups of such people for themselves are *physically challenged*, *differently abled*, and *handi-capable*. These terms acknowledge the difficulties. But the terms have the "attitude" that the person has the power to overcome the difficulties. They may be able to have a completely useful life, hold down a job, and contribute to the community. It's true that they may need wheelchairs, braces, artificial limbs, or hearing aids. But they do not need pity. Sometimes their name for others is *temporarily able*. This term reminds us that accidents happen, and disability can strike anyone.

Half of the human race is female. But women have only recently gained some political equality with men. The Declaration of Independence said "All men are created equal." Did this include women? Not really. In 1776, women could not own property, vote, or manage their own affairs. The unequal status was in the laws, and actually "built into" the English language itself.

People were referred to as *man*kind. The pronouns *he*, *him*, and *his* were used for "male or female" when the sex of the person referred to was not known. Words such as *mailman*, *fireman*, *policeman*, and *congressman* implied that these jobs were reserved for men only (and they were). Help Wanted columns in the newspapers were divided into two sections, Men and Women.

The following are some of the major changes that are occurring in the English language. If you listen to different people speaking, you will hear some using the "politically correct" terms, others using the "traditional" terms.

Politically Incorrect	**Politically Correct**
(When the gender of the person is not known:)	
he	he or she; she or he
him	him or her; her or him
his	his or her; her or his

Before 1980: "Anyone who wants help should write *his* name on the list. A volunteer will call *him* within a week." (This was supposed to refer to either a male or a female, using the male pronoun only.)

Now: "Anyone who wants help should write *his or her* name on the list. A volunteer will call *him or her* within a week." (Now women can be sure they are included.)

Now: To avoid having to repeat *he or she*, *his or her*, or *him or her*, you can just switch to the plural or to the second person (you) where the meaning will still be clear: "All those who want help should write their names on the list. A volunteer will call them within a week." Or, "If you want help, write your name on the list. A volunteer will call you within a week."

Various occupation names have been changed so that they may refer to either men or women.

Politically Incorrect	**Politically Correct**
fireman	fire fighter
policeman	police officer
mailman	letter carrier
salesman	salesperson
chairman	chair, chairperson
congressman	congressperson, representative

You can use the specific term when you know the gender of the person: "Steve Roth is a *congressman* from New Jersey." "Marge Roukema is a *congresswoman* from New Jersey." But if you don't know, use the gender-neutral term: "Who is the *congressperson* from your district?" "Sixty new *police officers* were hired."

(When referring to the entire human race:)

Man	humans, human beings
mankind	human beings

(When writing a letter to an unknown person:)

Dear Sir:	Dear Sir or Madam: Dear Person:

(When writing to a person whose name you know, but whose gender is uncertain:)

Dear Mr. Jones:	Dear M. Jones: Dear Leslie Jones:

Politically Incorrect	Politically Correct
retarded mentally handicapped	learning-disabled
slow learner failing student	underachiever
crippled, handicapped	physically challenged
dumb	mute
fat, obese, corpulent overweight	heavy, plump, chubby zaftig, Rubenesque
old old man, old woman	mature, elderly senior citizen "experienced" citizen
oldster, old-timer, aged	retired person
geriatric set	mature Americans golden agers
old maid	unmarried woman career woman
unwed mother	single mom, single parent
senile person	Alzheimer's victim
garbage collector garbageman	sanitation worker
janitor	custodian building caretaker, super
housewife	homemaker domestic engineer

Politically Incorrect	Politically Correct
girl (for a female over age 18)	woman
lady	woman
homo	gay, lesbian
deaf	hearing-impaired
crazy, mental, insane psychotic, disturbed	dysfunctional
short	compact diminutive petite (female)
bum bag lady	homeless person
broken home	single-parent family

Children of divorce were often referred to as coming from a "broken home." Now they have either a *single mom* or a *single dad*, and come from *single-parent families*.

Comedians have a lot of fun with people who insist on political correctness. They have made additional suggestions. These bring a smile, and make us wonder if "politically correct" terms will last.

poor	financially challenged
short	vertically challenged
dead	biologically challenged, differently existing

Some human actions are painful to talk about–such as dying. *Euphemisms* are terms used in order not to cause pain. *Slang* terms are used to defend against the pain. Use the clear term when you are talking about people or events that are not likely to disturb or upset the people you are talking to. "George Washington *died* in 1799." Use a euphemism to soften the meaning when emotion is recent or close in the family. "I was sorry to hear that your grandmother *passed away* last month."

clear term	die
euphemism	pass away, pass on, expire, go to heaven, go to meet one's maker, be called by the Lord, pass over to the other side, give up the spirit, cross over the great divide, go to one's rest, succumb, breathe his (or her) last, go to a better world
slang	croak, kick the bucket, buy the farm, cash in one's chips

clear term	dead person, cadaver
euphemism	dear departed, loved one, late lamented, decedent, last remains
slang	croaker, goner, stiff

clear term	graveyard, cemetery
euphemism	final resting-place, last home, memorial park
slang	bone orchard, cold storage

clear term	buried
euphemism	put to rest
slang	planted; six feet under, pushing up daisies

Discussion

1. How many of the "politically incorrect" terms were you taught in your English textbooks? (How long ago were the textbooks written?)

2. Is this kind of label-changing occurring in your native country?

3. What difference does it make what we call someone? Give examples.

4. In your language, are there pronouns for the different sexes? Is the male pronoun used when the gender of a person is not known? Have there been changes in the use of pronouns in your language?

5. Do you think the changes in English will help people to accept each other? Do you hear people using the new terms? Have you read them in newspapers and books?

True Stories of Dangerous English

D.P. was a fifty-year-old research scientist. He liked to ride a bike to work. He was riding his bicycle on a highway when a car passed him. In the car, there were some rough-looking characters, who yelled at him to get off the road. He "gave them the finger." (That is, he held up his middle finger in a vulgar insult.) They drove on.

A mile up the road, however, the same car was now parked. The men were waiting for him. They stopped him, knocked him off his bicycle, and beat him. "That's for the finger," said the driver. They left him badly injured by the side of the road.

U.M. was a college professor who was getting a divorce from his wife. It was a "nasty" divorce. U.M. thought that the judge was extremely incompetent. The judge's decision favored the wife, and U.M. was going to have to pay her a lot of his future salary. After the divorce, he sent postcards to both his ex-wife and the judge. He wrote, in vulgar terms, what he wished would happen to them. He was arrested, and put into jail for eighteen months. U.M. had thought that there was freedom of speech in America. But there is a law against "using the mail to threaten harm to another person." The judge decided that the vulgar language was a threat, and that U.M. had broken the law.

In 1970, hundreds of college students were protesting the war in Vietnam on the college campus of Kent State University in Ohio. They were good kids, and they believed they were doing the right thing. The National Guard was called out to preserve the peace. These young soldiers were good kids, too. Their job was to keep order. The students taunted and cursed the guards. The guards fired their rifles at the group of advancing students. Four students were killed. Later, there was an investigation. Why did young Americans shoot at and kill other young Americans? Part of the reason was lack of the troops' training. Another part was the language the protesters used. Even girls screamed abusive terms such as *mother fucker*, and *cock sucker*, at the soldiers. This made the angry students sound fierce, vulgar, and "un-American" to the soldiers. The language infuriated them. They lost their self-control.

President Nixon tape-recorded everything that he and others said in his office at the White House. During a Senate investigation of wrongdoing (the Watergate hearings), the tape recordings were discovered. The tapes were played. A written transcript appeared in the *New York Times*. Some of the words were unprintable, because they were vulgar. Wherever the President had said a vulgar word, the transcript read "expletive deleted." (vulgar word erased) Most adults could easily imagine which vulgar words the president and his staff had said. Many people were very shocked that such language was used in almost every sentence. (Other people were not shocked, because they know that this language is very common among men.) President Nixon was already in trouble. The transcript of his bad language did not help. He lost some of the respect and support he had from religious people. Serious crimes were discovered, and Nixon resigned.

Mark Fuhrman was a police detective with the Los Angeles Police Department. He was investigating the murder of O.J. Simpson's ex-wife, Nicole Simpson, and her friend Ron Goldman. Fuhrman discovered two bloody gloves-one near the dead bodies and one (Furhman said) at O.J. Simpson's home.

O.J. Simpson was a well-known black football player, actor, and TV sports commentator. The bloody glove, plus other strong evidence, seemed to prove that he had murdered the two people. But O.J.'s defense lawyer wanted to show that the policeman was a racist who did not like black people. He asked Detective Fuhrman, "Did you ever say the N-word?" (nigger). Detective Fuhrman said, on the witness stand (where he had promised to tell the truth), that he had never said "the N-word." But someone brought a tape recording and played it for the judge. It was a tape of detective Fuhrman saying *nigger* many times. He had lied. The jury decided that there was a reasonable doubt that this glove was Simpson's. They thought that a policeman who said "nigger" was a racist. He was capable of trying to make Simpson look guilty. The jury found Simpson not guilty. However, later, a different kind of jury listened to the main facts, and they decided that Simpson *had* killed his wife. But Simpson could not be sent to jail because he had been freed by the first jury. They could only make him pay a huge amount of money to the families of his victims.

Reverend Jesse Louis Jackson is a black activist and an eloquent speaker. He was a candidate for president in 1988. At a private meeting some years before, he had called New York City "Heimie Town." He meant that there were many Jewish people living there. Reporters learned that he had said that. They put this on the six o'clock TV and radio news and in the front pages of the papers. Jewish people and others were very offended. They called Jesse Jackson anti-Semitic (a person who hates Jews). Jackson lost the support of many Jewish people. Later, Jackson said that he did not know that the word *Heimie* was offensive to Jews. He apologized. But it was too late.

Judge Clarence Thomas was nominated for the Supreme Court of the United States. The Senate had to approve of his nomination. A committee of senators held a hearing about Thomas' abilities and character. A former worker in Thomas' office, Anita Hill, went before the committee to complain about him. Hill said that when she worked for Thomas ten years before, he had sexually harassed her. He had used vulgar language, shown her dirty pictures, talked about his sexual abilities, complimented her body, and invited her on dates, she claimed.

Many people all over the country thought that if this was true, Thomas was a bad candidate for the Supreme Court. Day after day, senators asked him questions about his language and his behavior. Anita Hill, who was a lawyer, said that she had been afraid to complain. The newspapers and TV reports told every detail of the testimony. Thomas was finally approved as a Justice of the Supreme Court. But it will be a long time before Americans can forget the things he was accused of. Because of this case, many women began to complain about the way men treated them at work. This was the beginning of laws against sexual harassment on the job.

In one case in San Francisco, quite a few years ago, a robber went into a bank to steal some money. He walked up to the female teller and said, "Give me all your fucking money." The teller was so upset about hearing the word fucking, that she took out the money drawer and hit the robber over the head with it. He was hurt so badly that he could not get away, and the police arrested him. Later, they asked the teller why she hadn't just given him the money. "When there's a holdup, we're supposed to give the robbers the money, so we don't get killed," said the teller. "It's the bank's policy. I would have given it to him. But when he used that terrible word, I got too angry. He shouldn't have used that terrible word."

Nike, the sports-shoe company had a small design on the back of their new shoes. This design looked like the word *Allah* in Arabic. Using the name Allah this way is forbidden in the Muslim religion. A fundamentalist Muslim saw the design. He told everyone all over the Islamic countries. The Islamic leaders threatened to boycott Nike if they sold the shoes with the design on them. There was a big protest, and Nike promised to destroy 38,000 pairs of shoes.

D.L. was a superintendent of schools in a small town in New Jersey. Many families in the town were Italian. D.L. made a comment about an Italian parent at a meeting of the board of education: "I suppose he'll put out a contract on me." This implied that the parent, being Italian, was also a member of the Mafia, and would hire someone to kill her for disagreeing with him. D.L. was joking and thought it was funny. It was extremely offensive to the Italian community. D.L. had to make a public apology. She said that she did not know that this was offensive. For this comment and other reasons, her contract was not renewed.

Discussion:

1. What stories can you tell about your own encounters with Dangerous English?

2. In your native language, what dangers have people gotten into?

Dangerous Synonyms and Related Words

In this section, you'll see the wide variety of terms that a single sexual body part or act might have. All of the words in each group are synonyms. Each refers to the same thing, but each also has its own social class and "attitude." People react differently to the different words. To learn more about each word and how it is used, check the Definitions Section.

The Human Body

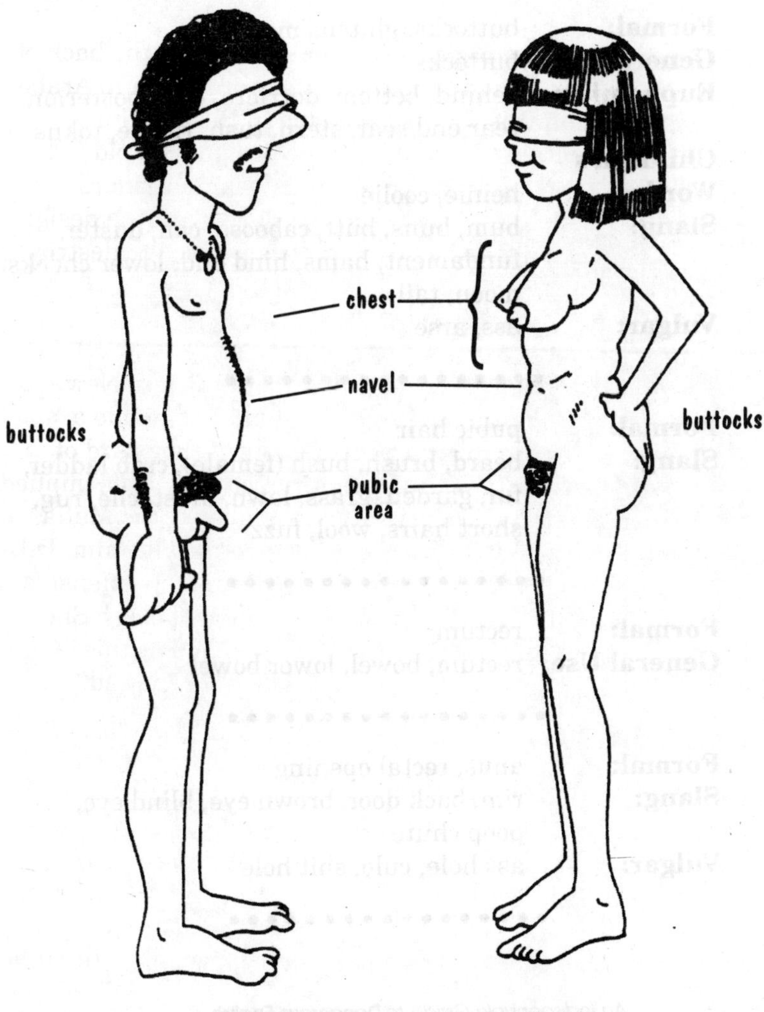

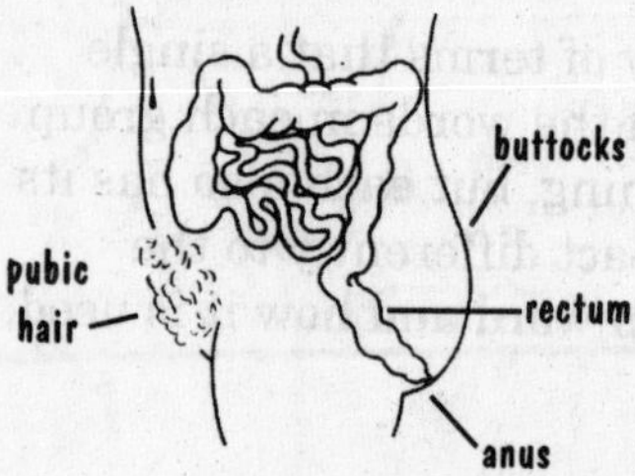

Formal: pubic area, genitalia, groin, urogenitals
General Use: sex organs
Euphemism: crotch, down there, the groin area, loins, private parts, privates, natural parts, secret parts

• • • • • • • • • • • • • • • • •

Formal: buttocks, gluteus maximus
General Use: buttocks
Euphemism: behind, bottom, derriere, duff, posterior, rear end seat, stern, tush, tushie, tokus
Children's Words: heinie, coolie
Slang: bum, buns, butt, caboose, can, duster, fundament, hams, hind end, lower cheeks, moon, tail
Vulgar: ass, arse

• • • • • • • • • • • • • • • • •

Formal: pubic hair
Slang: beard, brush, bush (female), crab ladder, fur, garden, grass, lawn, mustache, rug, short hairs, wool, fuzz

• • • • • • • • • • • • • • • • •

Formal: rectum
General Use: rectum, bowel, lower bowel

• • • • • • • • • • • • • • • • •

Formal: anus, rectal opening
Slang: rim, back door, brown eye, blind eye, poop chute
Vulgar: ass hole, culo, shit hole

• • • • • • • • • • • • • • • • •

The Human Body: Male

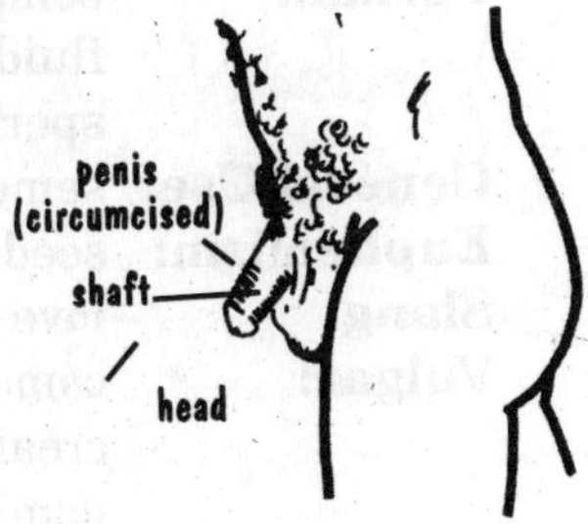

Formal: penis, male organ

General Use: penis

Euphemism: apparatus, male member, member, "it," you-know-what

Children's Words: thing, pee pee, peter

Slang: banana, bald-headed hermit, baloney, bird, carrot, cucumber, cue stick, John Henry, Johnson, lap lizard, one-eyed worm, pickle, pipe, short arm, sugar stick, thing, trouser trout

Vulgar: bone, bicho, cock, dick, dipstick, doodle, dork, dingus, hammer, horn, knob, joint, joystick, meat, pecker, peter, pork, prick, putz, ramrod, root, schlong, shaft, snake, tool, whang, wanger, wick, zipper monster

• • • • • • • • • • • • • • • • •

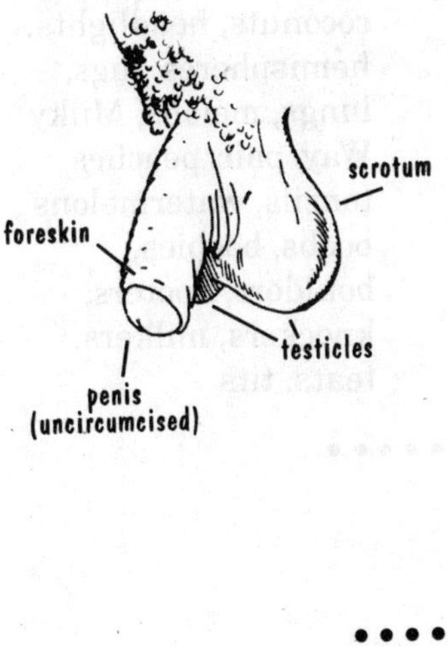

Formal: testicles, testes, male gonads

General Use: testicles

Euphemism: delicate parts of the anatomy

Children's Words: ballies

Slang: apples, cohones, family jewels, equipment, Rocky Mountain oysters

Vulgar: balls, knockers, 'nads (gonads), nuts, rocks, stones

• • • • • • • • • • • • • • • • •

Formal:	semen, seminal fluid, spermatozoa
General Use:	semen, sperm
Euphemism:	seed
Slang:	love juice
Vulgar:	come, cum, cream, jism, jizz

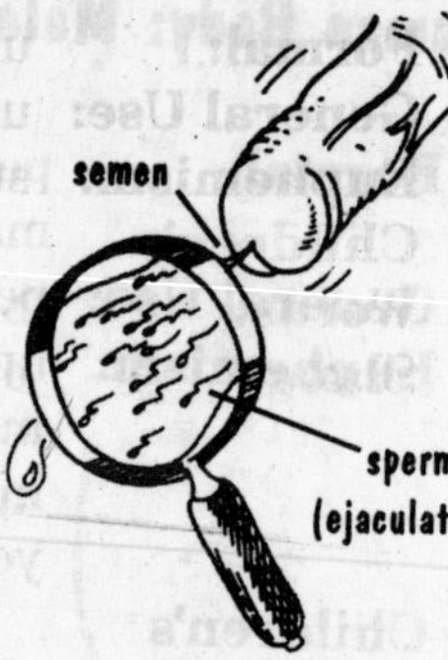

• • • • • • • • • • • • • • • •

The Human Body: Female

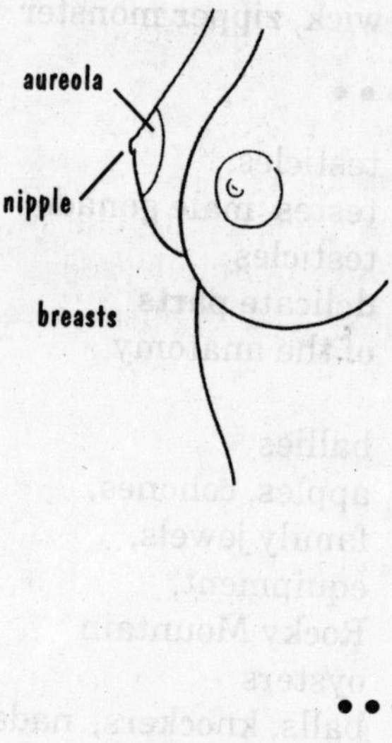

Formal:	breasts, mammary glands
General Use:	breasts
Euphemism:	bosom, bust, chest, front
Children's Words:	bubbies, pillows, titties
Slang:	apples, balloons, bazonkers, beauts, coconuts, headlights, hemispheres, jugs, lungs, melons, Milky Way, pair, peaches, tonsils, watermelons
Vulgar:	boobs, boobies, boulders, hooters, knockers, milkers, teats, tits

• • • • • • • • • • • • • • • •

Formal: uterus
General Use: uterus, womb
Euphemism: stomach
Children's Words: belly, tummy
Slang: oven, pot

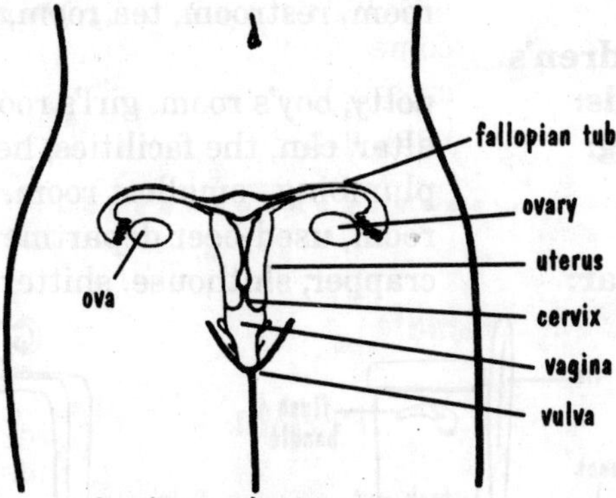

female reproductive organs

• • • • • • • • • • • • • • • •

Formal: vagina, birth canal, vulva, labia majora, labia minora
General Use: vagina, birth canal
Euphemism: down there, private parts
Vulgar: ass, bearded clam, beaver, box, clit, chocha, crack, cunt, hair pie, hole, manhole, meat, muff, mound, piece, pussy, slit, snatch, twat

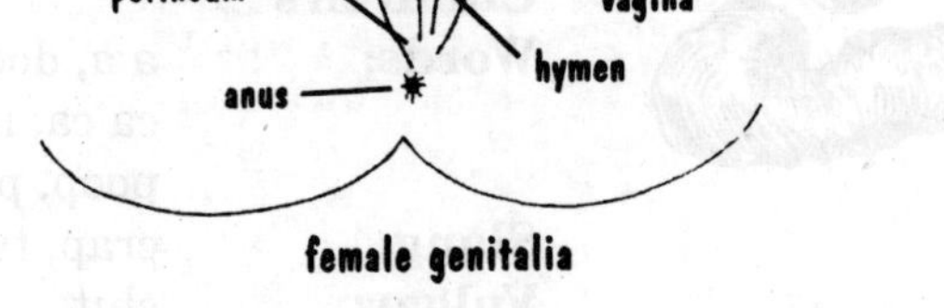

female genitalia

• • • • • • • • • • • • • • • • •

In the Bathroom

Formal: sanitary facilities
General Use: bathroom, toilet
Euphemism: (in public places): comfort station, ladies' (men's) room, lavatory, lounge, powder room, restroom, tea room, washroom
Children's Words: potty, boy's room, girl's room
Slang: altar, can, the facilities, head, john, library, plumbing, smallest room, throne, throne room, used-beer department
Vulgar: crapper, shithouse, shitter

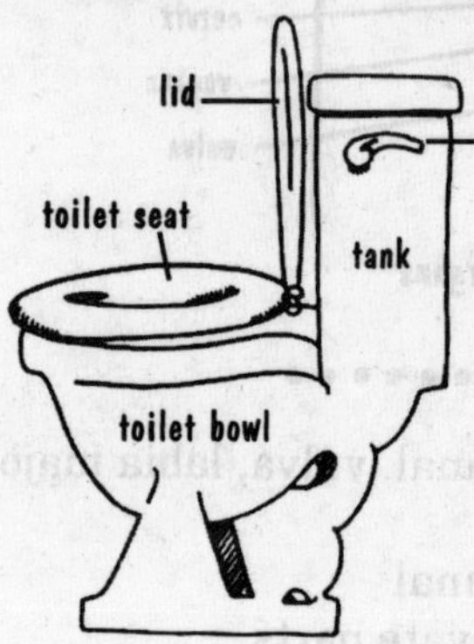

• • • • • • • • • • • • • • • • •

Formal: feces, fecal matter, excrement, stool
General Use: bowel movement
Euphemism: B.M., waste material, dirt, doo (dogs or cats)
Children's Words: a a, doodoo, doody, ca ca, number two, poop, poopoo, poozie
Slang: crap, turds, logs
Vulgar: shit

• • • • • • • • • • • • • • • • •

Formal:	defecate, move one's bowels, have a bowel movement, evacuate
General Use:	have a bowel movement
Euphemism:	go to the bathroom, go, make, eliminate
Children's Words:	go, make, or do: a a, eh eh, doodoo, doody, ca ca, number two, poop, poopoo, poozie
Slang:	feed the fish, use the facilities, see a man about a horse
Vulgar:	crap, dump, dump a load, pinch a loaf, shit, take a crap, take a dump, take a shit

• • • • • • • • • • • • • • • •

Formal:	diarrhea
General Use:	diarrhea, loose bowels
Slang:	the runs, the trots, the quickstep, Montezuma's revenge, *touristas*
Vulgar:	Hershey squirts, the shits

• • • • • • • • • • • • • • • •

Formal: constipation, be constipated
General Use: constipation, be irregular
Euphemism: irregularity, be irregular, unable to go
Children's Words: can't poop, can't ca ca
Slang: stuck, blocked up
Vulgar: shitting a brick

• • • • • • • • • • • • • • • •

Formal: be flatulent, expel gas
General Use: expel gas, pass gas
Euphemism: pass wind, break wind
Children's Words: make poops, go oops, poop
Slang: back talk, beep, blow the horn, buck snort, let one out, let out a stinker, let out a whiffer, winder, toot
Vulgar: blow a fart, blow one, cut a fart, cut one, fart, let out an S.B.D. (silent but deadly), rip one

• • • • • • • • • • • • • • • •

Formal: urinate, empty one's bladder, void
General Use: urinate
Euphemism: answer nature's call, go to the bathroom, make water, pass water, relieve oneself
Children's Words: do, go, or make: number one, pee pee, wee wee go potty, make a river, piddle, pish, go pishie, tinkle, wet
Slang: check the plumbing, check the sandbox, drain a vein, make a pit stop, water the lilies (or bushes)
Vulgar: leak, pee, piss, take a leak, take a piss, shake hands with a friend, water one's pony

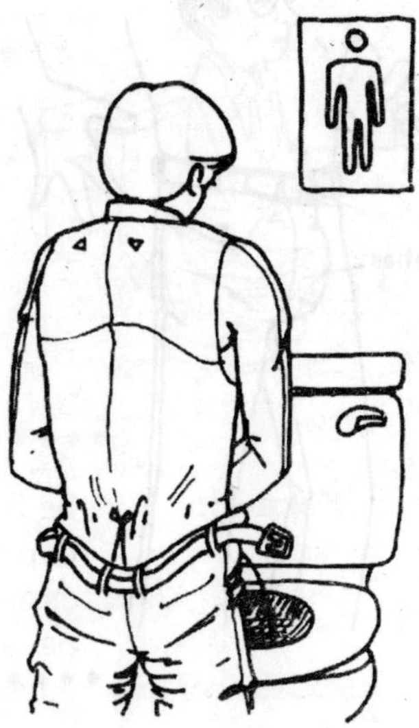

••••••••••••••••

Formal: menstruate (women only)
General Use: have one's period
Euphemism: that time of month, be unwell (out dated), "those days"
Slang have the curse (out dated), have one's friend, have the painters in, have a visit from Aunt Minnie
Vulgar have the rag on, be riding the cotton pony

••••••••••••••••

In the Bedroom

Formal:	have an erection, be erect
General Use:	be aroused, be excited
Euphemism:	be in the mood, be interested, be ready
Slang:	be hot, be hot and bothered, be hot to trot, have the hots, have lead in one's pencil, be turned on
Vulgar:	be horny, have a hard on, be hard, be stiff, have a boner, have a bone on

• • • • • • • • • • • • • • • •

Formal:	be lubricating
General Use:	be aroused, be excited
Euphemism:	be in the mood, be interested, be ready
Slang:	be juicy, be wet, be hot to trot, be turned on
Vulgar:	be horny, be ready for Freddy

• • • • • • • • • • • • • • • •

Formal:	copulate (with), have coitus, have (sexual) intercourse, engage in sexual intercourse
General Use:	have (sexual) relations, have sex, make love, mate (with)
Euphemism:	go to bed with, sleep with, have contact with, go all the way, have carnal knowledge of, know, be intimate with, couple, enjoy each other, possess
Slang:	diddle, do it, do the dirty deed, get down with, get a little, get some action, get it on, get with, have some, jump one's bones, make (a person), make it with, mess around, play fun and games, play "hide the sausage," roll in the hay, score

Vulgar:	ball, bang, dip (or wet) one's wick, frig, fuck, get into someone's pants, get laid, get one's end wet, get a piece of ass, get some ass, get some nookie, get some poon tang, get some pussy, hump, lay, schtup, screw, shaft, tear off a piece

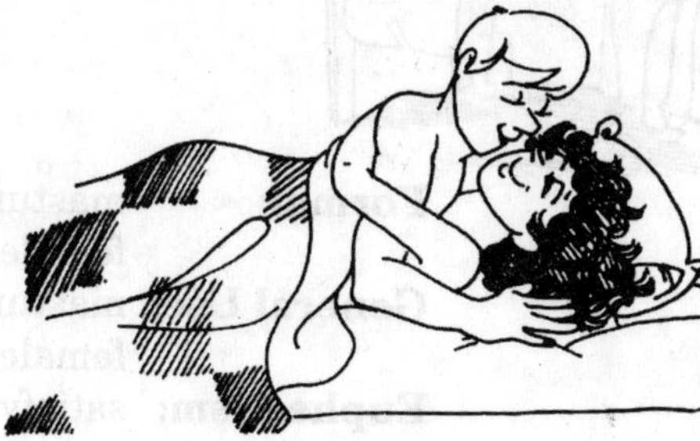

• • • • • • • • • • • • • • • •

Formal:	achieve orgasm, reach a sexual climax, ejaculate (male)
General Use:	have a climax, have an orgasm
Euphemism:	be satisfied, finish
Slang:	cream, drop one's cookies, get one's rocks off, get one's ashes hauled
Vulgar:	come, cum, drop one's load, get one's nuts off, give a shot, shoot off, shoot one's wad

• • • • • • • • • • • • • • • •

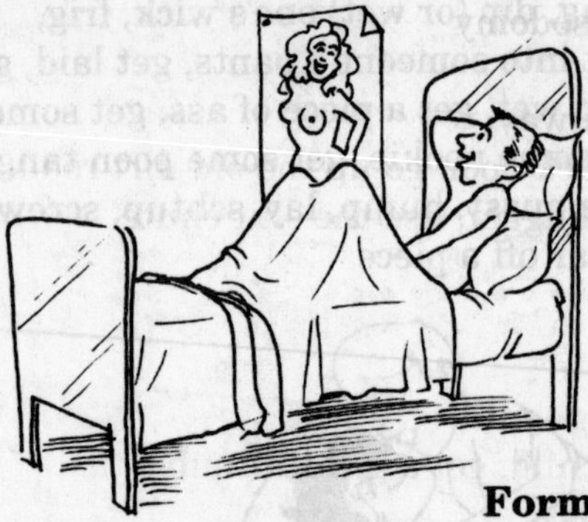

Formal: masturbate (male *or* female)
General Use: masturbate (male *or* female)
Euphemism: satisfy oneself, abuse oneself
Slang: diddle, play with oneself, see Madam Hand and her five daughters
Vulgar: beat the meat, beat off, choke the chicken, flog one's dong, fuck one's fist, jack off, jerk off, whack off, yank off (all male uses)

•••••••••••••••

Formal: oral-genital sex, (both sexes), fellatio (mouth to male genitals), cunnilingus (mouth to female genitals)
General Use: oral sex
Euphemism: go down on
Slang: sixty-nine, soixante-neuf (French)
Vulgar: blow, eat, give a blow job, give face, give head, go muff-diving, have hair pie, suck, suck cock, suck dick

•••••••••••••••

Formal:	anal sex, sodomy
General Use:	anal sex
Euphemism:	the Greek way
Slang:	use the back door, go up the old dirt road
Vulgar:	ass-fuck, bugger, use the shit chute

• • • • • • • • • • • • • • • •

Formal:	impregnate
General Use:	make pregnant
Euphemism:	get with child, get a girl in trouble (if unmarried)
Slang:	plant a watermelon seed in her belly
Vulgar:	knock up

• • • • • • • • • • • • • • • •

Formal:	pregnant, gestating
General Use:	pregnant
Euphemism:	great with child, in a family way, expecting a child
Slang:	preggers, swallowed a watermelon seed, have one in the oven, cooking one in the pot
Vulgar:	knocked up

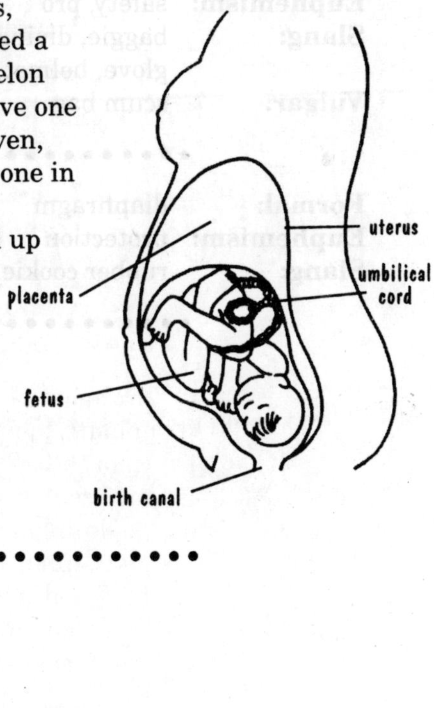

• • • • • • • • • • • • • • • •

Formal: contraception, (use) contraceptive devices
General Use: (use) birth control, spermicidal jelly tube
Euphemism: be safe, be careful, (take) preventive measures, (take) precautions
Slang: make the playground safe for play

• • • • • • • • • • • • • • • •

Formal: condom, prophylactic
General Use: condom
Euphemism: safety, pro
Slang: baggie, diving suit, envelope, French letter, glove, helmet, overcoat, raincoat, rubber
Vulgar: scum bag

• • • • • • • • • • • • • • • •

Formal: diaphragm
Euphemism: protection
Slang: rubber cookie, catcher's mitt

• • • • • • • • • • • • • • • •

On the Street

Formal: heterosexual
General Use: heterosexual
Slang: straight

Formal: homosexual (either sex), lesbian (female)
General Use: gay (either sex), homosexual (male), lesbian (female)
Euphemism: the third sex, "hairdresser," "decorator"
Slang: (derogatory:) homo, neuter gender, person of indeterminate gender, queer, queen, fairy, fruit, pansy
(derogatory, female:) butch, dyke, bulldyke, lezzie, sugar plum fairy, fag, faggot
Vulgar: cocksucker, buggerer (male), dick smoker, fudge packer, pickle chuggler, salami smuggler (all derogatory)

Formal: prostitute
General Use: prostitute, street walker, call girl
Euphemism: lady of the night, lady of easy virtue
Slang: flesh peddler, harlot, hooker, hustler, tart, paid lady, princess of the pavement, working girl
Vulgar: ass peddler, cunt-for-sale, slut, ho, whore

Formal: male prostitute (heterosexual)
General Use: gigolo
Euphemism: escort service
Slang: midnight cowboy

Formal: male prostitute (homosexual)
General use: hustler
Euphemism: "on the street"
Slang: chicken, retail queen
Vulgar: slut, rental unit

Formal: house of prostitution
General Use: house of prostitution, brothel
Euphemism: bordello, disorderly house, house of ill repute, house of pleasure, joy house, massage parlor, red-light district
Slang: bawdy house, cat house, flesh market, meat house, sporting house
Vulgar: fuckery, fuck house, whore house

Dangerous People: Perverts and Perversions

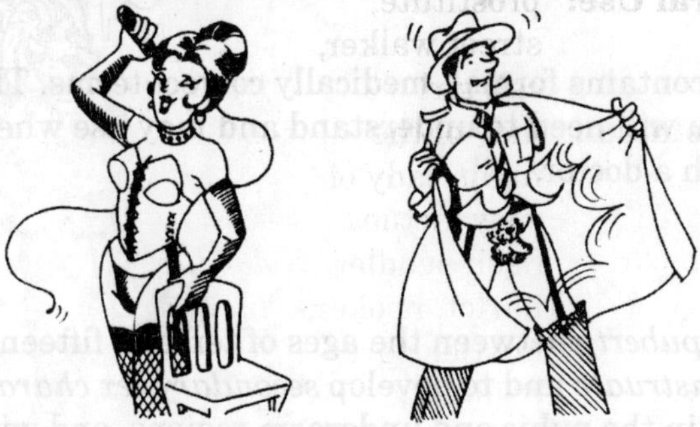

A perversion is a sexual act that is not "normal." There are religious rules against "non-normal" sex practices. In some states, there are also civil laws.

Today, people object to laws that reach into their private bedrooms. They feel that "consenting adults" (consenting = giving permission freely, not forced) should be free to engage in any sex practice they choose in the privacy of their bedrooms.

But sex practices that harm children or *nonconsenting adults* are considered serious crimes by everyone.

Definitions of the terms below are given in the Definitions Section on pages 109 to 195.

Deviation	Deviant
bestiality	
buggery	buggerer
exhibitionism	exhibitionist/flasher
fetishism	fetishist
molestation	molester/child molester
masochism	masochist
necrophilia	necrophiliac
pederasty	pederast
pedophilia	pedophile
rape	rapist
sadism	sadist
sado-masochism	sado-masochist
sodomy	sodomist
transvestism	transvestite (TV)
voyeurism	voyeur/peeping Tom

Dangerous English Goes to the Doctor

This section contains formal, medically correct terms. These are the terms you will need to understand and may use when speaking with a doctor.

Females

A girl enters *puberty* between the ages of ten and fifteen. She begins to *menstruate* and to develop *secondary sex characteristics*: breasts, hair in the pubic and underarm regions, and wider hips. The female *hormones–estrogen* and *progesterone*–cause these body changes.

Each month, an *ovum* (egg) leaves the *ovary*. It passes through the *fallopian tubes* to the *uterus*, and out of the *vagina*. The thick lining of the *uterus* is released, and *menstruation* occurs. The woman says she is *having her period*.

Problems that some women have are *heavy flow*, *menstrual cramps*, and an *irregular cycle*. Some women experience *P.M.S. (Premenstrual Syndrome)* for a few days before their period. They feel bloated, crampy, and irritable.

A woman will use a *sanitary napkin* to absorb the *menstrual flow*. Or, she may insert a *tampon* into the vagina.

Toxic shock syndrome is a rare, but very dangerous, condition. It can be caused by bacteria that build in the vagina. This can happen when a woman leaves a tampon in too long. A high fever, dizziness, headache, and other symptoms may occur.

Before her first *sexual experience*, a girl is a *virgin*. There is a *hymen* (a thin membrane) that partly covers the opening to the vagina. This will stretch or tear during her first *sexual intercourse*. Sometimes it will tear before this if the girl is active in such sports as tennis, volleyball, or running hurdles.

A *gynecologist* is a doctor who specializes in treating conditions of women's *reproductive* organs.

A visit to the gynecologist will include a breast examination and a *pelvic* examination. The doctor may also do a *Pap Smear*, a *urinalysis*, and check for *vaginal itch*, *vaginal discharge*, or other signs of *vaginitis*. He or she may check for a *sexually transmitted disease (STD)*, and may recommend medication, a change in diet, or a *douche*. The doctor can also teach the woman how to do a *breast self-examination* to feel for lumps that might be cancerous.

When a girl or woman becomes *sexually active*, she can discuss *birth control* with the gynecologist. The doctor will explain how birth-control pills, a *diaphragm*, *spermicidal foam*, or an *intra-uterine device* work. The doctor will explain that *douching* is not effective, nor is *coitus interruptus* (withdrawal during intercourse). If the patient does not want to use artificial birth control for any reason, the doctor will explain the *rhythm method*, or other natural forms of birth control (which are usually less effective).

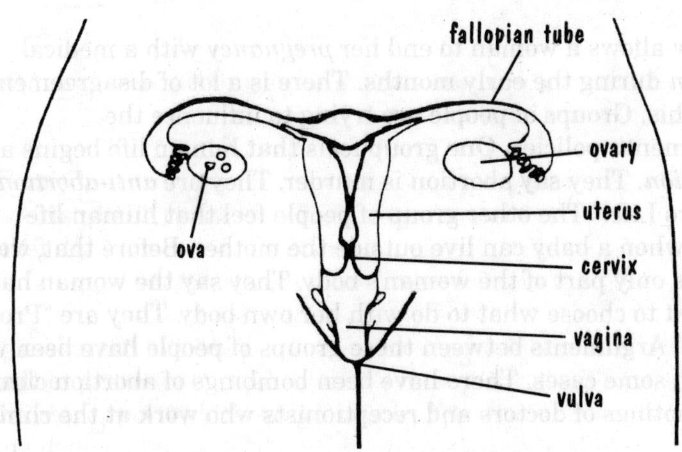

So far, the only 100% effective methods of birth control are *abstinence* and *sterilization*. If a woman has already had several children, she may think about "having her tubes tied." This is called a *tubal ligation*. The fallopian tubes either are cut or they are closed and sealed. Then the ova (eggs) cannot reach the uterus.

An *obstetrician* is a doctor who cares for women during pregnancy, and assists at the baby's delivery. Most gynecologists are also obstetricians. Some women prefer to give birth to a baby at home. A *midwife* is a person who is trained to help with home-based deliveries.

If a woman experiences *painful intercourse*, the doctor may advise a *lubricant*, such as K-Y Jelly™.

If a woman's ovum is *fertilized* by her partner's *sperm*, it begins to grow. It then attaches itself to the lining of the *uterus*. The woman misses her period, which may or may not be her first sign that she is *pregnant*.

Another early sign of pregnancy may be "morning sickness." The *fetus*, or unborn child, usually will *gestate* for nine months. One in six pregnancies ends in *miscarriage*.

The law allows a woman to end her *pregnancy* with a medical *abortion* during the early months. There is a lot of disagreement about this. Groups of people are trying to influence the government's policies. One group feels that human life begins at *conception*. They say abortion is murder. They are *anti-abortion* and "Pro Life." The other group of people feel that human life begins when a baby can live outside the mother. Before that, they say, it is only part of the woman's body. They say the woman has the right to choose what to do with her own body. They are "Pro Choice." Arguments between these groups of people have been very fierce in some cases. There have been bombings of abortion clinics, and shootings of doctors and receptionists who work at the clinics.

Labor contractions begin when the baby is ready to be born. If the birth is very difficult, the doctor may decide to do a *caesarian section*. This is an operation to remove the baby from the uterus.

After the baby is born, the mother may *breast-feed* her baby, or bottle-feed it. She may do *Kegel exercises* to strengthen the muscles in her vagina.

A married couple who are unable to *conceive* may go to an *infertility clinic*. The doctors there may recommend *artificial insemination*, or the use of a *sperm donor*.

Some other concerns of women are intermittent bleeding, staining, and painful *ovulation*. Women also may have *endometriosis*, burning during urination, and hormonal imbalances. *Fibrocystic breast conditions* are normal in many mature women. They may be painful, and even confused with cancer. A *mammography* is a special kind of X-ray for breast cancer. If cancer exists, a woman may need a *mastectomy* (removal of the breast) or a *lumpectomy* (removal of the lump or tumor).

A woman's *childbearing* ability may end around age forty-five to fifty. Her ovaries stop producing estrogen. She undergoes *menopause*, or the "change of life." Her periods become *irregular*, and then stop. She may have *hot flashes*. These may make her feel as though someone just turned up the heat. Some doctors recommend *estrogen replacement therapy*, or *hormone* treatments for difficulties that may come with menopause. Other doctors prescribe natural herbs to deal with hot flashes.

Postmenopausal bleeding can be serious. Sometimes all that is needed is a "D and C" (dilation and curettage). The gynecologist cleans the lining of the uterus. There may be a need for a *hysterectomy*, or removal of the uterus by surgery. Women are advised to always get at least a second opinion (that is, consult a second, or even a third, doctor before deciding what to do).

Males

Today, many baby boys in the U.S. are *circumcised* a few days after birth. This means that part of the *foreskin* of the *penis* is cut off.

Doctors in favor of circumcision say that it makes it easier to clean the baby's penis. *Smegma* collects under the foreskin. If it is not cleaned off, infection can result. Other doctors say the penis is easy to clean, so there is no need for circumcision. This operation is becoming less popular. Parents are asking: Why is it necessary to hurt a child? Why take away something he was born with?

In Jewish families, circumcision has a religious meaning. The circumcision is a ceremony, called a *bris*, to dedicate the boy to God.

A young boy starts to become an adult between ages eleven and sixteen. This time is called *puberty*. A boy's testes produce the male *hormone*, called *testosterone*. Testosterone causes the boy's body to change. He begins to have the *secondary sex characteristics* of males. His muscles grow larger. His voice gets deeper. A beard begins to grow on his face. Hair grows under his arms, on his chest, and in the *pubic area*. At night he may have *nocturnal emissions* ("wet dreams").

When a boy plays in sports, he will need to wear a *jock strap* or a *protective cup* to avoid injury to his *genitals*.

A family doctor can treat many medical conditions of men. For special cases a man might go to a *urologist*. A urologist specializes in treating the *urogenital tract*. Male problems may include difficulty *urinating*, or too-frequent urinating, blood in the *urine*, or blood in the *semen*.

Small stones can form in the kidneys. These *kidney stones* may cause pain when they are passed from the kidneys to the *bladder*. They may cause pain again when they pass from the bladder through the *urethra*.

A *catheter* may be needed when there is difficulty urinating. This goes through the urethra to the bladder. A *cystoscope* allows a doctor to look into the bladder.

A strange *discharge* from the penis may mean infection or be a symptom of a *sexually transmitted disease*.

Occasionally a *testicle* does not descend before birth. An undescended testicle is a problem that may need surgery or *hormone* treatments.

A *hydrocoele* is a fluid-filled sac that may form in the *scrotum*. *Epididymitis* or *orchitis* are painful infections of the scrotum that require immediate treatment. Self-examination of the testicles (TSE) is recommended to detect small lumps early.
A *straddle injury* occurs when the testicles have been hurt from either a fall or a kick in the groin. "Jock itch" is a *fungus* in the pubic region.

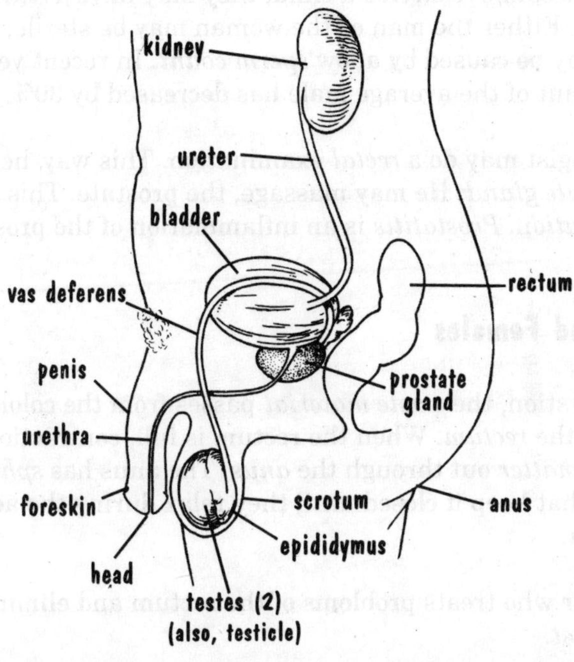

A *hernia* occurs when a part of the intestine breaks through a thin part of the lining of the abdominal wall. Men are more likely to get hernias than are women. There is a weak place in the *groin* (crotch). Hernias can develop either slowly, or suddenly during heavy lifting or straining.

A man may have sexual difficulties. He may ask the doctor about *impotence*. This condition stops him from having an *erection* so he cannot complete the sex act. A man may have decreased *libido*, or have "*performance anxiety*." He experiences *premature ejaculation* if he comes to *orgasm* before he wants to, during sex. The doctor may recommend an appointment with a *sex therapist*.

Priapism is a disease condition causing the penis to stay in a state of erection. It is the subject of jokes, but is really a painful condition.

A *penile implant* is a device inserted in the penis. This can help a man have an erection, so he can engage in sexual intercourse.

If a couple cannot *conceive* a child, they may have *fertility* problems. Either the man or the woman may be sterile. *Sterility* in a man may be caused by a low *sperm count*. In recent years, the sperm count of the average male has decreased by 30%.

The urologist may do a *rectal* examination. This way, he can check the *prostate gland*. He may massage, the prostate. This will cause an *ejaculation*. *Prostatitis* is an inflammation of the prostate.

Males and Females

After digestion, the *waste material* passes from the colon and is stored in the *rectum*. When the rectum is full, contractions push the *fecal matter* out through the *anus*. The anus has *sphincter muscles* that keep it closed until they relax during the act of *defecation*.

The doctor who treats problems of the rectum and elimination is a *proctologist*.

Common conditions and complaints of the rectum and anus are: *constipation*, *hard stools*, *bloody stools*, *black stools*, *soft stools*, *straining at stool*, *flatulence (gas)*, *cramps (pain)*, *diarrhea (loose, runny stools)*, *hemorrhoids*, *colitis*, *irritable-bowel syndrome (spastic colon)*, *colo-rectal cancer*, *anal itching*, and anal pain. The anus may develop painful *fissures*.

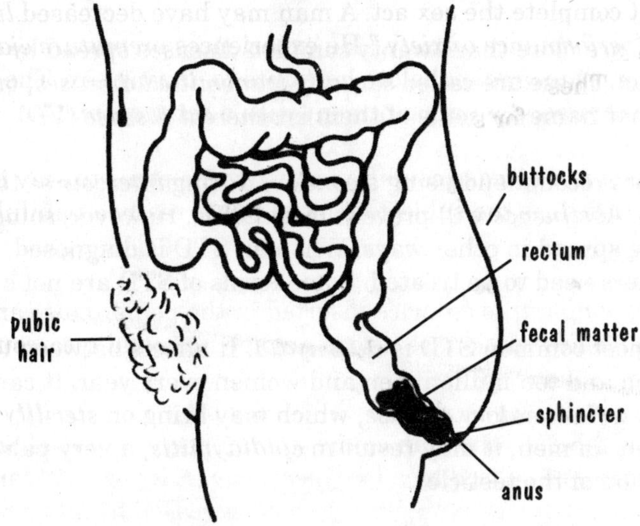

To diagnose some conditions, the doctor may do a *sphygmoidoscopy*. This means inserting a long, flexible instrument into the rectum, in order to look inside the colon. Another test the doctor may do is take X-rays after the patient has had a barium *enema*. He or she may also test the stool for blood.

Other problems may be *rectal polyps* (small growths in the lining of the rectum), anal or rectal fissures (cracks in the skin), fistula *rectocele*, and rectal *prolapse* (an intrusion of the rectum through the anus). *Proctitis* is an infection of the rectum. There are several causes, but it may be sexually transmitted through anal intercourse.

Recommendations may be high-fiber diets, *sitz baths*, *stool softeners*, medication, or surgery.

Sexually Transmitted Diseases (STD's)

There are more than twenty common diseases spread by sexual contact. These are called *sexually transmitted diseases*, or *STD's*. Another name for some of them is *venereal disease (VD)*.

Doctors recommend using a *condom* during *intercourse* to prevent STDs. *Abstinence* will prevent most STDs. However, some of them can be spread in other ways. When an STD is diagnosed, *both* partners need to be treated. Some forms of STD are not curable.

The most common STD is *chlamydia*. It affects between four million and ten million men and women every year. It can cause *pelvic inflammatory disease*, which may bring on *sterility* in women. In men, it may result in *epididymitis*, a very painful infection of the testicles.

A common infection transmitted sexually is *candida*, also called a *yeast infection*. A parasite called *trichomonas* is also sexually transmitted. *Syphilis* is a dangerous STD that used to kill many people. If it is not treated it can enter the heart, the brain, and other vital organs. (Fortunately, one large dose of antibiotics can stop it.) The first symptom is a hard lump around the genitals that becomes an open sore. But not everyone gets the sore, so syphilis can be a silent killer. It may be detected by blood tests. Many states require blood tests for syphilis before granting a marriage license.

The symptoms of *gonorrhea* are a thick creamy *discharge* of white or yellow pus from the penis, urethra, or vagina. An infected person will want to urinate often. Urination will feel painful, and the urine will be cloudy. If it is not treated, gonorrhea can cause infertility, arthritis, and infections of the heart and brain.

Herpes is a virus that affects about one-fourth of the adult sexually-active population. A half-million men and women get it every year. There are several kinds of herpes virus. Herpes sores can appear on the mouth or on the *genitals*. Genital herpes can be spread through sexual contact. It can also be spread from toilet seats, trying on others' bathing suits, using someone's towel or washcloth, or sharing a hot tub.

AIDS is caused by the HIV virus. This virus can be spread through sexual contact, especially anal sex. It can also be spread by drug users who share needles. People have also gotten HIV from blood transfusions in hospitals. Babies of mothers with AIDS usually are born with the virus, too.

A *wart* is a small hard bump on the skin. Genital warts can be spread through sexual contact.

Pubic lice, commonly called *crabs*, can be spread through sexual contact. You can also get them from a toilet seat, trying on others' bathing suits, sharing a towel or the same bed with a person who has them. A person may not know he or she has them until after several weeks of itching and scratching.

Dangerous Definitions and Sample Sentences

Stop! You will find this section easier after you learn the formal words that are illustrated on pages 81-97. Many definitions here will refer to those correct terms.

In a book of this size, we cannot include every medical, slang, or vulgar word for sexual or toilet activities. (One researcher found over 1,200 words for sexual intercourse alone!) We have chosen over 800 of the words and expressions you are most likely to hear, or need to use. These are words that are commonly known by many Americans in most parts of the country. (Women are likely to know fewer of these words than men.)

Be careful: Not all of the meanings of the words are dangerous. We do not have the space to give every possible meaning for each word. We include only the meanings that are related to sex, to toilet acts and functions, and to expressions that include these words.

For example, a standard dictionary gives twenty-eight meanings for the word *head*. You probably know many of the meanings. In this book, we explain only the sex-related slang and vulgar meanings.

What does the star (*) before certain words mean?

Some words have only a dangerous meaning. Other words have both dangerous and safe meanings. Those words that have additional meanings that we do not refer to here are marked with the (*). If you don't already know the common meaning of the word, you may look it up in a standard dictionary or your bilingual dictionary.

Remember, the meaning of words depends on the context of the conversation. Words that are said with affection or humor can mean something very different from the same words spoken in anger.

Remember also that the listener is the person who decides what words mean to him or her. An angry person will find angry meanings even when the speaker intended to be funny or friendly.

A

*__abstinence__ ('æb stɪ nəns) noun. formal and general use. Not having sexual relations. From the verb *abstain* (to choose *not* to have or do something. "Schools teach *abstinence* as the only sure way to avoid pregnancy."

*__accident__ ('æk sɪ dənt) noun. 1. slang euphemism. An unplanned baby. A failure of birth control. "Our first child was planned, but the other two were *accidents*." 2. euphemism. A bowel movement or urinating in one's pants. "Our three-year-old daughter is toilet-trained, but she has an *accident* now and then."

*__a.c./d.c.__ ('ei siː 'diː siː) adj. slang. Bisexual. This is said of a person who has sexual relations with both men and women. (The reference is to two different kinds of electrical current: alternating current and direct current.) "Kay is *a.c./d.c.*"

*__adult__ (ə 'dʌlt) adj. euphemism. For people over eighteen years of age. When the word *adult* is used in the expressions *adult bookstore*, *adult movies*, and *adult entertainment*, it has the meaning: for adults only. It's about sex. (*Adult education* does *not* have this meaning!)

__adultery__ (ə 'dʌ l tə ri) noun. formal, legal, and general use. Sexual intercourse between a man and a woman who are not married to each other. At least one of the partners is married to someone else. The word includes the judgment that the act is wrong, or criminal. "In the Christian religion, *adultery* is a sin." "Mrs. C. wanted a divorce because her husband had committed *adultery*."

__adulterer__ (ə 'dʌl tə rər) noun. formal. A person who commits adultery.

__adulteress__ (ə 'dʌl trɛs) noun. formal. A woman who commits adultery.

__adulterous__ (ə 'dʌl tər əs) adj. formal. "Does *adulterous* behavior make a man unfit to be President?" asked Marcie.

The words *adultery*, *adulterer*, *adulteress*, and *adulterous* are not related in meaning to the word adult.

* words with additional meanings not listed

*__affair__ (ə 'fɛər) noun. general use. A sexual relationship between a man and a woman who are not married to each other. The word does not carry a judgment of right or wrong. "Amy had many *affairs* before she got married."

AIDS (eidz) noun. formal and general use. A disease, Auto-Immune Deficiency Syndrome. It is caused by the HIV virus. This disease weakens a person, so he or she may easily die from other diseases. HIV is spread through unprotected sex, particularly anal intercourse; through sharing hypodermic needles, as drug addicts might do; and through transfusions of AIDS-contaminated blood during surgery. "Babies born to mothers with *AIDS* also have the HIV virus."

A.K. (ei kei) noun. 1. Euphemism for the vulgar term *ass-kisser*. (see) 2. vulgar. *alte koche*. A Yiddish expression that means "old shitter," or a "dirty old man" who likes to flirt with or romance pretty young women.

*__alley cat__ ('æ liː 'kæt) noun. slang. A man or woman who has casual sexual relations with many people. "Nick was a real *alley cat* before he got married, but he's been faithful to his wife since then."

*__all the way__ ('ɔːl ðə 'wei) adverbial phrase. Euphemism commonly used by teenagers. To go "all the way" means to have complete sexual intercourse. *Half way* may mean kissing, necking, and petting (touching the genitals). "Clara was afraid of sex, so she never went *all the way* with a boy."

*__altar__ ('ɔl tər) noun. slang. The toilet.

*__alter__ ('ɔl tər) adverbial phrase. euphemism. To remove the sex glands (testicles or ovaries) of a cat, dog, or farm animal so it cannot reproduce. "We had our cat *altered*." Synonym: *neutered*. A male animal is *castrated*, while a female animal is *spayed*.

*__altogether, in the__ (ın ðə ɔːl tə 'gɛð ər) phrase. euphemism. Naked; with no clothes on. "Sheila took off her wet clothes and stood by the fire *in the altogether*."

A

anus ('ei nəs) noun. formal and medical use. The exit hole of the rectum. "The feces (digestive waste material) are pushed out of the body through the *anus*."

anal sex ('ei nəl 'sɛks) noun. formal. Sexual intercourse in the anus.

***arouse** (ə 'raʊz) verb. general use. Cause someone to become sexually excited. "Rita's gentle kisses *aroused* Marty." "Some men get *aroused* when they see bare breasts."

arse (ɑːrs) noun. vulgar. The buttocks.

ass (æs) noun. general use. A foolish person. This is a short form of the word *jackass*, a male donkey. This use of the word is not vulgar, although many people will no longer use it in polite company.

ass noun. vulgar. 1. The buttocks. 2. The rectum. 3. The anus. 4. The vagina.

There are many expressions that include the word ass.

ass-backwards ('æs bæk wərdz) adj., adverb. vulgar. Backwards, all mixed up. Done in a confused way. Also *bass ackwards*. "These directions are all *ass-backwards*; I can't understand what to do." "Hank does everything *ass-backwards*."

ass hole ('æs houl) noun. vulgar. 1. The anus. 2. A stupid person. "Those *ass holes* down in Washington are ruining the country!" he complained.

ass-hole buddy ('æs houl 'bʌd i) noun. vulgar. A very close friend. (Not homosexual, as the term might make you think.) "Roger, George, and Sam and I were *ass-hole buddies* all through college."

ass-kisser ('æs kɪs ər) noun. vulgar. A person who is overly nice to a boss, teacher, or supervisor. He or she wants special privileges, good marks, or favors. "Bob is the biggest *ass-kisser* I know. He's always telling the boss what a great boss he is." Also, **A.K.**

* words with additional meanings not listed

ass man ('æs mæn) noun. vulgar. 1. A man who finds the buttocks to be the most sexually attractive part of a woman or man. 2. A man who is constantly interested in sex, in finding new sex partners, and in talking about his sexual adventures.

ass peddler ('æs pɛd lər) noun. vulgar. A prostitute (male or female). To peddle one's ass is to sell sexual services. "D. came to the big city to become an actress, but she wound up being an *ass peddler*."

ass-wipe ('æs waɪp) noun. vulgar. 1. Toilet paper. 2. A very stupid person.

bare-ass, bare-assed ('bɛər æs, 'bɛər æst) adj. vulgar. Completely naked. With no clothes on. "The boys went swimming *bare-ass*." "He opened the dressing-room door and caught her *bare-assed*."

bust one's ass (bʌst wʌnz 'æs) verb phrase. vulgar. 1. To work very hard to accomplish a goal. "L. *busted his ass* to finish the job before Friday." 2. Punish by forcefully spanking the buttocks. "If you do that again, I'll *bust your ass*!" shouted the angry mother to the child.

dumb ass ('dʌm æs) noun phrase. vulgar. A stupid person.

get one's ass in gear (gɛt wʌnz 'æs ɪn giər) verb phrase. vulgar. To get organized. "We made a lot of mistakes at first, but as soon as we got our ass in gear, we got results."

half-assed ('hæf æst) adj. vulgar. 1. Done in a sloppy, inefficient manner. "Who did this *half-assed* job?" yelled the boss. 2. Stupid, lazy. "How did I ever hire such a *half-assed* worker?"

haul ass (hɔːl 'æs) verb phrase. vulgar. To hurry. "It's ten to eight, we'd better haul ass if we want to get there on time."

have lead in one's ass (hæv 'lɛd ɪn wʌnz 'æs) verb phrase. vulgar. To be very slow-moving. (Lead is a very heavy metal.) "Hurry up, Joe! What's the matter–you got *lead in your ass*?" "Get the *lead out of your asses*, boys; we've got to finish this job by 5 p.m."

kick ass (kɪk 'æs) verb phrase. vulgar. To get tough; to threaten people; to demand results or rapid work. "A construction foreman has to be able to *kick ass* when it's necessary."

ass, to kiss (kɪs 'æs) verb. vulgar. To continually compliment and do favors for a superior, hoping for a promotion, good marks in class, or special favors. "You don't have to know anything in Professor Bruce's class. All you have to do is *kiss ass*: Tell him how interesting his course is."

not know one's ass from one's elbow (nɑt nou wʌnz æs frʌm wʌnz 'ɛl bou) verb phrase. vulgar. To be unaware, stupid, uninformed, ignorant. "How can Charlie be the supervisor of that company? He doesn't *know his ass from his elbow*." (Also: ...**from a hole in the ground**.)

pain in the ass (pein ɪn ðə 'æs) noun. vulgar. 1. A very irritating person or problem. "That neighbor is *a real pain in the ass*. She never stops complaining." 2. Something that is very annoying. "That job was *a pain in the ass*. There were many small parts that had to be fixed."

piece of ass (piːs əv 'æs) noun. vulgar. 1. An act of sexual intercourse. (Here, ass here means vagina.) "Karl went around to all the bars looking for *a piece of ass*." 2. A woman, regarded as a sexual object only. "Donna looks like *a great piece of ass to me*," said Ed.

Shove it up your ass! Up your ass! Up yours! (ʃʌv ɪt ʌp yər 'æs; 'ʌp yər 'æs; 'ʌp 'yʊrz) Angry statements. vulgar. They may refer to someone's argument, apology, merchandise, gift, advice, or complaint. Also: Stick it up your ass; Shove it. "You know what you can do with it" is a euphemism for "Shove it up your ass."

smart-ass ('smɑːrt æs) noun. vulgar. 1. A person who acts as if he or she knows everything; a "know-it-all." 2. A sarcastic person. Also, **wise-ass**. "Jeff is a real *smart-ass*."

tight-ass ('taɪt æs) noun. vulgar. A person who is overly concerned with correct behavior, small details, and following the rules as carefully as possible. He or she may also be stingy, emotionally cold, and prudish. "Professor Lawson is a real *tight-ass*. He asks questions about the smallest details; no one ever gets an 'A' in his course."

You bet your sweet ass (yuː 'bɛt yər swiːt 'æs) vulgar expression. You can be sure of it. "Are you going to ask for your money back?" asked Jose. "*You bet your sweet ass* I am," said Derek.

athletic supporter (æθ 'lɛ tɪc sə 'pɔːr tər) noun. euphemism. Jock strap. A garment worn by male athletes or workers, to protect the genitals from getting hurt.

B

***back door** (bæk 'dɔːr) noun. slang. The anus.

backside ('bæk saɪd) noun. euphemism. The buttocks.

bad ass ('bæd æs) adj. vulgar. Good.

***bag** (bæg) noun. slang. The scrotum.

***baggie** (bæ gi) noun. slang. A condom.

bald-headed hermit ('bɑld 'hɛd id 'hɛr mɪt) noun. slang. The penis. (A hermit is a person who lives alone. Bald = Without hair on his head.)

B

*__ball__ (bɔːl) verb. vulgar. Have sexual intercourse. "They *balled* all night." To have a sexual relationship with. "Marie was *balling* her boss all summer, but no one in the office knew about it."

ball-buster ('bɔːl bʌs tər) noun. vulgar. 1. A very difficult job; a boss or other person who is hard to please. "The test was a real *ball-buster*. I couldn't finish it in the two hours we had. "Professor B. is a real *ball-buster*. He wants students to read six chapters of the text a week, and write three term papers." 2. An attractive woman who seems hard to please. "Look at the girl in the low-cut dress. I bet she's a real *ball-buster*." 3. A woman who causes a man to lose his sense of masculinity.

*__ball and chain__ (bɔːl ən 'tʃein) noun. slang. A wife. (This is not a vulgar term. Prisoners on an outdoor work project used to be chained to a heavy lead ball so they would not run away. Being married is compared to being a prisoner who cannot have any freedom.)

*__balls__ (bɔːlz) noun, plural. vulgar. 1. The testicles. 2. Masculine courage; nerve, daring. "That lion tamer certainly *has a lot of balls* to go into the cage with six lions." "*It takes balls* to say what you think when everyone disagrees with you." "Devin was working for the company only six weeks. Then he asked for a 10% raise. *That takes balls.*"

balls, to have someone by the (tə hæv sʌm wən baɪ ðə bɔːlz) verb phrase. vulgar. To have power to force someone to do what is wanted. "Rick wanted to break up with his girlfriend, but *she had him by the balls*. She owned the business he worked for."

ballsy ('bɔːl zi) adj. vulgar. Courageous. Having masculine courage. (This may be said of women, too, nowadays.) "He's quite *ballsy*, isn't he, to fight a crocodile with his bare hands."

*__bang__ (bæŋ) verb. vulgar. To have sexual intercourse.

bare-ass ('bɛər æs) adj. vulgar. Naked. Also **bare-assed**. "There was no one around, so we went swimming *bare-assed.*"

bar-girl, B-girl ('bɑːr gəːrl, 'biː gərl) noun. slang. An attractive woman who works in a bar. Her job is to encourage customers to spend more money. She behaves in a friendly, sexually inviting manner, and the customer buys drinks for her. The customer does not know that she is an employee of the bar. The bartender fills her glass with tea or colored water, and charges the price of liquor. A bar-girl may also sell sexual services, as a prostitute.

***basket** ('bæs kət) noun. slang. 1. A woman's genitals. 2. A man's genitals. The shape of the man's genitals that can be seen in tight clothing.

basket days ('bæs kət deiz) noun, plural. slang. Warm weather. The shape of men's genitals can be seen because they are wearing light clothing, such as shorts, bathing suits, tight jeans, etc. (homosexual use)

bastard ('bæs tərd) noun. 1. vulgar. A very disliked person. "Ralph is a real *bastard*. He deserted his wife and three kids and took all of their money out of the bank, too." 2. vulgar. *Bastard* may be used in a joking way to refer to a good friend. "Mike, you old *bastard*, I haven't seen you in a long time! Where've you been?" 3. The original meaning of bastard is *an illegitimate child* (a child born to an unmarried woman.)

bathroom ('bæθ ruːm) noun. general use. A room with a toilet. There may also be a bath tub and a sink. The word bathroom used to be a euphemism. (When you go to the bathroom you are not really going there to take a bath!)

bathroom tissue ('bæθ ruːm 'tɪ ʃyuː) noun. euphemism and general use. Toilet paper. A roll of soft tissue paper used in the bathroom. The companies that make this paper label it "bathroom tissue" or "toilet tissue." Most Americans call it **toilet paper**.

*__beard__ (biərd) noun. slang. 1. Male facial hair 2. Female pubic hair. 3. A homosexual or straight male who goes to social events as the "date" of a lesbian. "She did not want her colleagues to think she was a lesbian, so she took Joe to the convention as a *beard*."

bearded clam (biər did 'klæm) noun. vulgar. The external genitals of a woman.

beat off (biːt 'ɔːf) verb. vulgar. Masturbate. "A lot of guys *beat off* after seeing a sexy movie."

beat the meat (biːt ðə 'miːt) verb phrase. vulgar. Masturbate.

*__beauts__ (byuːts) noun, plural. slang. A woman's breasts.

*__beaver__ (biː vər) noun. vulgar. A woman's pubic area. The vagina.

*__beaver patrol__ (biː vər pə 'troul) noun phrase. vulgar. Looking for women, especially women who might be wearing shorts or mini-skirts.

bed; go to bed with (gou tə 'bɛd wɪθ) verb phrase. euphemism. Have sexual intercourse with. "Larry used to *go to bed* with every girl he dated."

bedpan ('bɛd pæn) noun. general use. In a hospital, a plastic or metal pan for patients to urinate or defecate into when they are not able to get out of bed to go to the bathroom.

bedroom eyes ('bɛd ruːm 'aɪz) noun. general use. Large, sexy-looking eyes. Eyes in which the pupils are enlarged, indicating a state of sexual arousal.

bed-wetter ('bɛd wɛt ər) noun. general use. A child who wets (urinates) in bed while sleeping at an age when this "mistake" is not expected (past four years old).

*__behind__ (bə 'haɪnd) noun. euphemism. The buttocks.

belly-button ('bɛ liː 'bʌ tən) noun. general use and children's word. The navel.

*__bestiality__ (biːs tʃiː 'æ lə ti) noun. formal. 1. Sexual relations between a human being and some other ("lower") animal. 2. Sodomy.

between the sheets (bə 'twiːn ðə ʃiːts) noun. euphemism. In bed; the place where people have sexual intercourse. "What goes on with me and my wife *between the sheets* is none of anybody else's business," said Fred.

*__bicho__ ('bi tʃou) noun. vulgar. Penis. (from Spanish vulgar slang)

bidet (biː 'dei) noun. general use. A small washstand that a woman can sit on, and so wash the genital area easily. Widely used in Europe, especially France.

birds and bees (bərdz ən biːz) idiom. euphemism. The facts about how babies are started. In the past, many parents were too embarrassed to explain sex to their children. Instead, they told them how flowers and birds reproduce. "Well, little Jimmy asked where babies come from. I guess it's time he learned about the *birds and the bees*."

birth control ('bərθ kən 'troul) noun. general use. A way to prevent getting pregnant. "If a person is going to have sexual relations, he or she should first know about *birth control*." "What *birth-control* method did your doctor recommend?"

birthday suit ('bərθ dei suːt) noun. euphemism. One's skin, without any clothes on. "The swimmers were wearing nothing but their *birthday suits*."

bisexual (baɪ 'sɛk ʃuːəl) noun. formal and general use. A person who enjoys sexual relations with both males and females. Also used as an adjective. "Did you know that Sean is *bisexual*? He's married and the father of two kids, but he has his boyfriends, too." Also **bi**

B

bitch (bɪtʃ) noun. slang. 1. An unpleasant, complaining and demanding woman. 2. A sexy and attractive woman. 3. verb. slang. To complain. "Marty is always *bitching* about his job." Original general use and formal meaning: *a female dog*.

bitchy ('bɪtʃ i) adj. slang. Easily irritated; crabby and complaining.

son of a bitch (sʌn əv ə bɪtʃ) noun. vulgar. Literally, the son of a female dog. 1. A selfish, hateful person who causes unhappiness for others. "Mr. Arthur is a real *son of a bitch*. He would sell his own grandmother if he could make a profit from that." 2. A very difficult, time-consuming job. "Trying to move that heavy piano was a real *son of a bitch*." 3. An expression to show surprise at an unexpected happening. "*Son of a bitch*! I never expected to see you here in Miami!" 4. Affectionate term for a good friend. "Hi, you *old son of a bitch*; it's good to see you." **S.O.B.** is the abbreviation, which is less vulgar.

bladder ('blæ dər) noun. formal and medical use. The organ that holds urine until the waste liquid leaves the body.

blind eye (blaɪnd 'aɪː) noun. slang. The anus.

***blow** (blou) verb. vulgar. Give sexual pleasure by sucking the penis orally (in the mouth). Perform *fellatio*.

***blocked up** (blɑkt 'ʌp) verb phrase. euphemism. Constipated.

blow a fart ('blou ə 'fɑːrt) verb phrase. vulgar. Expel gas from the rectum.

blow job (blou dʒɑb) noun. vulgar. Fellatio. The act of giving sexual pleasure by sucking a partner's penis.

blue balls ('bluː 'bɔlz) noun, plural. A pain in the testicles. Young men repeat the myth that this happens when a male who has been sexually aroused for a long time doesn't ejaculate. It may gain a girlfriend's sympathy.

* words with additional meanings not listed

B.O. (biː ou) noun. euphemism. A bad body odor (smell).

***bob** (bɑb) verb/noun. vulgar. Oral sex.

***boner** (bou nər) noun. vulgar. The penis, when it is erect. (have a) bone on: have an erection.

boobs; boobies ('buːbz, 'buː biːz) noun, plural. vulgar. Women's breasts.

booger ('bʊ gər) noun. vulgar slang. A lump of dried mucus from the nose. Also, children's words: **boogie, boogieman**. There is no polite English word in general use for this "product of picking one's nose."

bordello (bɔːr 'dɛ lou) noun. euphemism. House of prostitution.

bosom ('bʊ zəm) noun. euphemism. The breast area. "The child slept with his head on his mother's *bosom*." (A *bosom* friend is a good friend, *close to the heart*.)

***bottom** ('bɑt əm) noun. euphemism. The buttocks.

bowel movement ('baʊl muːv mənt) noun. formal and general use. The colon (lower part of the digestive tract) is sometimes called the *bowels*. To "move one's bowels" is to expel the waste products of digestion (the feces). "The baby had a *bowel movement* in his diaper." "Some doctors recommend prunes or bran cereal to help you *move your bowels*."

b.m. (biː ɛm) noun. euphemism. Bowel movement. To **have a b.m.; to make a b.m.** = *defecate*.

***box** (bɑks) noun. vulgar. The vagina.

***boxers** ('bɑk sərz) noun, plural. general use. Men's undershorts.

***box lunch** ('bɑks lʌntʃ) noun. vulgar. Cunnilingus or fellatio. Oral sex. Mouth-to-genitals sex.

***boy** (bɔɪ) noun. slang. This word may be extremely offensive when it is used by a white person when talking to or about a black male adult.

bra, brassiere (brɑː, brə ˈziər) noun. general use. An article of clothing that gives support to the breasts. "Her *bra* size is 36-C."

B

breast (brɛst) noun. general use. The upper chest area of either a man or a woman.

breasts (brɛsts) noun, plural. general use. The mammary glands. The female organs which produce milk for a newborn baby.

-breasted (-ˈbrɛs tid) adj. general use. Combined with *big*, or *small*, this is used to describe the size of the breasts. "She's a *big-breasted* woman."

breast feed (brɛst fiːd) verb. general use. Give a baby milk from the mother's breast. To nurse a baby. "Are you planning to *breast feed* your baby or bottle-feed it?" "Mrs. Jacobs *breast fed* all seven of her children."

***briefs** (briːfs) noun, plural. general use. Men's undershorts.

bris (brɪs) noun. formal and religious use. The circumcision of a Jewish baby boy seven days after birth. Family and friends are invited to a formal ceremony. The foreskin of the baby's penis is cut by a religious official called a mohel (mou həl). Then the family celebrates and has a party.

***Bronx cheer** (brɑnks ˈtʃiər) noun. slang. A loud passing of gas from the rectum, done on purpose to show contempt. A sound made by sticking the tongue out and expelling air around it. "He gave out a *Bronx cheer* to show that he did not care for our offer."

brothel (ˈbrɑ θəl) noun. formal. A house of prostitution.

***brown eye** (braʊn ˈaɪː) noun. slang. The anus.

***brush** (brʌʃ) noun. vulgar. A woman's pubic hair.

buck snort (ˈbʌk snɔːrt) noun. vulgar. A loud release of intestinal gas.

*__bugger__ ('bʌ gər) 1. verb. vulgar. To have sexual intercourse in the rectum. Commit sodomy. 2. noun. vulgar. A person who commits *buggery*. A homosexual.

buggery ('bʌ gə ri) noun. vulgar. The act of sexual intercourse in the rectum. *Sodomy*.

bulldyke ('bʊl daɪk) noun. vulgar. A lesbian who is mannish and aggressive. (derogatory)

bullshit ('bʊl ʃɪt) noun. vulgar. 1. The feces of bulls (male cattle). 2. A story or description that is not believable. Lies. "What Erik told you is a lot of *bullshit*. Don't believe him." 3. Meaningless sentences, stories, or facts. "Helen didn't know the answers to any of the questions on the examination, so she just wrote a whole lot of *bullshit* and hoped the professor would give her a passing grade." 4. verb. vulgar. To tell lies or false stories. To grossly exaggerate. "Don't let Paul *bullshit* you; he doesn't know what he's talking about." 5. To talk, argue, tell jokes, enjoy casual conversation among friends. "We sat around *bullshitting* until the bars closed.

*__bull__ (bʊl) noun. euphemism for bullshit. "You're full of *bull*." (I don't believe you.) "Don't *give me that bull*." (Don't lie to me.) **B.S.** (biː ɛs) = bullshit.

bullshit artist ('bʊl ʃɪt 'ɑːr tɪst) noun. vulgar. A person who tells unbelievable stories but gets other people to believe that the stories are true. "Gary would make a good salesman. He's quite a *bullshit artist*."

bum (bʌm) noun. slang. Buttocks.

Bumblefuck ('bʌm bəl fʌk) (also **Bumfuck**, **East Bumfuck**) U.S.A. noun. vulgar. A quiet, boring town in a farm area, where there is nothing interesting to do; "Nowheresville."

*__bumpers__ ('bʌm pərz) noun, plural. slang. A woman's breasts. (Cars have bumpers in front and back to soften the impact in case of an accident.)

*__bung hole__ ('bʌŋ houl) noun. vulgar. The anus.

C

***buns** (bʌnz) noun, plural. slang euphemism. The buttocks. "He has a nice pair of *buns*."

***bunny** ('bʌ ni) noun. slang. A loose woman. A male or female prostitute.

bunnyfuck ('bʌ ni fʌk) verb. vulgar. Very rapid intercourse.

***bush** (bʊʃ) noun. vulgar. A woman's pubic hair.

***business; to do one's business** (tə duː wʌnz 'bɪz nɛs) verb phrase. euphemism. To defecate, to urinate, to use the bathroom.

***bust** (bʌst) noun. general use. The breast area of a woman. This word is used in giving the measurements of the body and for clothing sizes. "Miss America has a thirty-six-inch *bust*, a twenty-five-inch waist, and thirty-eight-inch hips." "Blouses, brassieres, and bathing suits are generally marked with the *bust* size."

***butch** (bʊtʃ) noun. slang. A female homosexual who appears masculine in haircut, dress, or manner.

***butt** (bʌt) noun. slang. The buttocks. "I was ice-skating and fell on my *butt*."

buttocks ('bʌ ɒəks) noun. formal and general use. The fatty, muscular area of the lower back.

***button** ('bʌt ən) noun. slang. The clitoris. Also, **love button**.

C

ca ca ('kɑ kɑ) noun. children's word. Feces. **make ca ca.** verb phrase. Defecate.

call girl ('kɔl gərl) noun. general use. A high-priced prostitute. She works by appointment, not in a house of prostitution or on the street.

***camp** (kæmp) adj. slang. Gay.

camp as a row of tents ('kæmp æz ə 'rou əv 'tɛnts) adj. slang. Very clearly gay.

***can** (kæn) noun. slang. 1. The buttocks. "He fell on his *can*." 2. The bathroom. "Who's in the *can*? Hurry up! I have to go, too!"

carnal knowledge ('kɑːr nəl 'nɑ lədʒ) noun phrase. euphemism. Sexual intimacy.

castrate ('kæ streit) verb. formal and medical use. Remove the testicles by surgery. "Bulls are *castrated* so they will be easier to handle and the meat will be more tender." "Male cats are often *castrated* to prevent their habit of urinating on furniture." Synonyms: neuter, fix.

cat house ('kæt haʊs) noun. slang. A house of prostitution.

cervix ('sʌr vɪks) noun. medical use. The neck or opening of the uterus.

change of life (tʃeindʒ əv 'laɪf) noun. euphemism. The menopause in women. "My wife is going through *the change of life*. I guess we won't have any more children unless we adopt some." **the change** (ðə tʃeindʒ) = The change of life.

***cheap** (tʃiːp) adj. derogatory slang. Having low morals, dressing in poor taste, wearing too much makeup, easy for men to have sexual relations with, etc. "Look at that blonde. With the purple lipstick and the low-cut blouse, she sure looks *cheap*."

***cheat** (tʃiːt) verb. slang. To be unfaithful to one's husband, wife, or steady sex partner. To have sexual relations with another person without the knowledge of one's usual partner. To commit adultery. "Marcia *cheats* on her husband all the time." "Jordan never *cheats* on his girlfriend." noun. slang. A person who is not faithful to a lover or spouse. (*spouse* = husband or wife)

check the plumbing (tʃɛk ðə 'plʌ mɪŋ) verb phrase. slang euphemism. Go to the bathroom. "Excuse me. I'll be back as soon as I *check the plumbing*." Also, **inspect the plumbing**.

*__cheeks__ (tʃiːks) noun, plural. general use. The two round, fatty sections of the buttocks. Sometimes called the "lower cheeks" to distinguish from the face cheeks.

*__cherry__ ('tʃɛr i) noun. vulgar. 1. The hymen. The flap of skin that covers part of the vagina before a woman's first act of sexual intercourse. An unbroken hymen is considered to be a sign of virginity. 2. A virgin; an inexperienced person.

__bust a cherry__ (bʌst ə 'tʃɛr i) vulgar. To have sexual intercourse with a girl who is a virgin.

__lose one's cherry__ (luːz wʌnz 'tʃɛr i) vulgar. To have intercourse for the first time, losing one's virginity.

__still have a cherry__ (stɪl hæv ə 'tʃɛr i) vulgar. To be a virgin, a woman who has never had sexual intercourse.

*__chest__ (tʃɛst) noun. 1. general use. The front area of the body between the shoulders and the waist on either a man or a woman. 2. slang. The breasts of a woman.

__chi chi__ ('tʃiː tʃiː) adjective. slang. Gay.

*__chicken__ ('tʃi kən) noun. slang. A young male prostitute who sells sexual services to older male homosexuals.

*__chicken hawk__ ('tʃi kən hɔːk) noun. slang. A male homosexual who buys the sexual services of a young male prostitute.

__chicken shit__ ('tʃi kən ʃɪt) noun. vulgar. Something that is completely worthless, uninteresting and unrewarding. "What is this *chicken shit* you sold me?" Also used as an adjective. "Y. said he hated his *chicken-shit* job, so he was planning to quit."

__chocha__ ('tʃo tʃə) noun. vulgar. Vagina. (from the Spanish)

__choke the chicken__ ('tʃouk ðə 'tʃɪ kən) verb phrase. vulgar. Masturbate.

circumcision (sər kəm 'sɪ ʒən) noun. formal and general use. A surgical procedure to remove part of the foreskin of a baby boy's penis. It is done for religious or health reasons. "All Jewish baby boys are *circumcised* ('sər kəm saɪzd) seven days after birth." The formal ceremony to which family and friends are invited is called a *bris*.

***clap** (klæp) noun. vulgar. Gonorrhea, a venereal disease. A disease that is gotten through sexual contact with an infected person. (Used with the) "R. got *the clap* from a prostitute."

***climax** ('klai mæks) noun. formal and general use. 1. Orgasm. The moment of most intense pleasure during sexual intercourse. The male climax is when he ejaculates. A woman's climax is when there are rhythmic contractions in the vagina. 2. verb. "They *climaxed* together."

reach a climax (riːtʃ ə klai mæks) verb phrase. general use. Have an orgasm. "A man may *reach a climax* before his partner."

clitoris ('klɪt ər əs) noun. formal, medical, and general use. The small, highly sensitive organ that is located in the forward part of the vulva. This is the organ in the female that is responsible for much sexual pleasure and orgasm. adjective form: *clitoral*.

clit (klɪt) noun. vulgar. The clitoris.

closet case; closet queen ('klɑ zət keɪs, 'klɑ zət kwiːn) noun. slang. A male homosexual who does not act like a homosexual in public. His neighbors and co-workers may think he is heterosexual.

to come out of the closet (tə kʌm 'aʊt əv ðə 'klɑ zət) verb phrase. slang. To stop hiding one's homosexuality. To stop pretending in public to be a heterosexual. "When the Gay Liberation Movement began, thousands of gay men and women *came out of the closet*."

C

***coconuts** ('kou kə nʌts) noun, plural. slang. A woman's breasts.

***cock** (kɑk) noun. 1. vulgar. The penis. This is one of the most common terms used among men to refer to the male sex organ. 2. general use. A rooster (male chicken).

***cockpit** (kɑk pɪt) noun. vulgar. A woman's genitals.

cock sucker ('kɑk sʌk ər) noun. vulgar. Literally, a person who sucks cocks (performs fellatio); a male homosexual. The word is more often used as an insult to describe a hateful person. It is similar to, but much stronger than, the words *bastard* and *son of a bitch*.

cock tease ('kɑk tiːz) noun. vulgar. A woman who acts as though she were sexually interested in a man, but who will not have intercourse with him after he has become aroused. "Naomi has the reputation of being a *cock tease*."

***cod** (kɑd) noun. vulgar. Penis

cod piece (kɑd piːs) noun. general use. In medieval times, a covering for the penis that protected it and exaggerated its size.

cohabit (kou 'hæb ɪt) verb. formal and legal use. 1. To live together as man and wife. "They decided to get married after *cohabiting* for six years." 2. To have regular sexual relations when married.

coitus ('kou ɪ təs) noun. formal and medical use. Sexual intercourse. "During *coitus*, the blood pressure and pulse of both partners rises." "The average married couple in their twenties engages in *coitus* two to five times a week."

cojones; cohones (ko 'ho neis)/(kou 'hou niːz) noun, plural. vulgar. 1. Testicles. "Look at the *cojones* on that dog!" 2. Masculine courage. "It takes *cojones* to be in the Marines."

colorful language ('kʌ lər fəl 'læŋ gwɪdʒ) noun. general use and euphemism. Speech that is full of slang or vulgar expressions, or unusual ways of describing things. "Reading this book will help you to understand some *colorful language*."

***come; cum** (kʌm) 1. verb. slang. Have an orgasm or sexual climax. (In a male, *ejaculate*.) "Paul always *comes* three or four times before Ken *comes*." "Did you *come* yet?" (A common question by anxious lovers.) "I'm *c-c-c-coming*!" she moaned. 2. noun. slang. **cum**: The semen or vaginal fluid that is ejaculated during orgasm.

***come across** (kʌm 'ə krɔs) verb phrase. slang. To submit to a man's sexual advances. "Women don't *come across* so easy anymore," said Xavier. "I guess they're all afraid of getting AIDS."

come-hither look (kʌm 'hɪð ər 'lʊk)) noun. general use. An expression on a person's face that seems to say "I'm feeling passionate. Come here." "Glenda wore a loose-fitting robe and gave Jack that *come-hither look* that he could not resist."

comfort station ('kʌm fərt 'steɪ ʃən) noun. euphemism. A public bathroom, usually along a well-traveled highway.

commode (kʌ 'moud) noun. euphemism. A toilet.

***conceive** (kʌn 'siːv) verb. formal and general use. To become pregnant. "Tiffany has been trying to *conceive* ever since she got married."

***conception** (kʌn 'sɛp ʃən) noun. formal and medical use. The union of the male sex cell (sperm) with the female sex cell (ovum). "Some religions teach that a human life begins at the moment of *conception*."

condom ('kɑn dəm) noun. general use. A contraceptive worn by the male over the penis. It may be made of very thin rubber latex or the thin membrane of animal intestines. "The *condom* is 94% safe as a preventative of pregnancy."

constipated ('kɑn stə peit əd) adjective. formal and general use. Unable to defecate; having difficulty in passing stool. "Every time Ann ate cheese, she became *constipated*, and didn't have a bowel movement for days."

C

constipation ('kɑn stə pei ʃən) noun. formal and general use. Difficulty in moving one's bowels. "To avoid *constipation*, eat salads, raw fruits, and whole grains. Also, drink plenty of water."

contraception (kɑn trə 'sɛp ʃən) noun. formal. Methods of preventing pregnancy. Birth control. "Jean asked her doctor if there were any new forms of *contraception* that were more effective than 'the pill.'"

***coolie** ('kuː li) noun. children's word. euphemism. The buttocks.

copulate ('kɑp yu leit) verb. formal and medical use. Have sexual intercourse. "Most animals *copulate* less frequently than human beings."

***crabs** (kræbz) noun. plural. slang and general use. A certain kind of lice that live in the pubic hair of humans (also in underarm hair and beards). They are very tiny and extremely itchy. "*Crabs* can be caught from close personal contact, from sleeping in a bed or from sitting on a toilet that has been used by someone with *crabs*."

crab ladder ('kræb læ dər) noun. slang; humorous use. Some men have hair leading from the pubic area to the navel. This hair could supposedly be used by crabs (lice), if the person had them, to climb to the midsection of the body.

***crack** (kræk) noun. vulgar. The vagina.

***cramps** (kræmps) noun. plural. general use. Contractions of the intestine or uterus, causing pain. "Clarissa always gets *cramps* on the first day of her menstrual period."

* words with additional meanings not listed

***crap** (kræp) noun. vulgar. Feces. (synonym: *shit*) **Take a crap.** Defecate. **Full of crap.** vulgar. Full of lies and unbelievable stories. "Pete is *full of crap*. Don't follow his advice, whatever you do." Worthless things. "Why did you buy all that *crap*? You've wasted a lot of your money." "Mary ate lots of *crap*." (candy, soda, chocolate, beer, potato chips).

***cream** (kriːm) 1. noun. vulgar. Semen. 2. verb. vulgar. To ejaculate; to have an orgasm. **cream in one's jeans** verb phrase. vulgar. To ejaculate with one's pants still on. This is often an exaggerated way of saying that someone is very sexually aroused. "Philip nearly *creamed in his jeans* when Marla Mammalia walked into the room."

crotch (krɑtʃ) noun. general use. The pubic area. The angle formed by the two legs where they join the body. (A tree has a crotch, too.)

crotch rot ('krɑtʃ rɑt) noun. slang. Itchy, irritable skin in the crotch area; jock itch.

crud (krʌd) noun. slang. 1. Dried semen. 2. Any disgusting dirt or dried food.

***cucumber** ('kyu kʌm bər) noun. slang. 1. The penis. 2. An artificial penis, or a device to use for masturbation.

cuckold ('kʌk əld) 1. noun. slang. A husband whose wife has been unfaithful. 2. verb. slang. To make one's husband a cuckold by having sex with another man.

cunnilingus (kʌ nɪ 'lɪŋ gəs) noun. formal. Oral-genital contact. Stimulation of the female genitalia by the partner's tongue.

cunt (kʌnt) noun. vulgar. 1. The vagina. 2. A woman. (derogatory).

cuntlet ('kʌnt lɛt) noun. vulgar. A young girl. An attractive woman.

***curse** (kərs) verb. general use. 1. To use vulgar language. To swear. "Timothy was so angry he *cursed* for five minutes." 2. To ask God or the Devil to cause bad luck or injury to happen to someone or something. "We *cursed* the landlord for raising the rent." 3. noun. general use. Any vulgar word. "Marcus knows a lot of *curses* and he's only five years old." 4. Bad luck sent by God or the Devil or one's enemies. "Dillon blamed all of his bad luck on a *curse* that his enemies had put on him."

D

the curse (ðe kərs) noun. slang. The menstrual period. "Carla won't go swimming because she has the *curse*." (This word implies that the speaker has a negative feeling about this natural body function.)

***cut the cheese** (kʌt ðə 'tʃiːz) verb phrase. slang. To expel gas from the rectum. "Phew, what a smell! Who *cut the cheese*?"

cut a fart (kʌt ə 'fɑːrt) verb. vulgar. To expel gas from the rectum. Also: **cut one**. "Yolanda ate rice and beans for lunch and she's been *cutting farts* all afternoon."

D

damn! damn it! (dæm, dæm ɪt) verb, interjection. vulgar. An expression of anger or disappointment. **God damn it!** vulgar. Expression of extreme irritation or anger. "*Damn you*! I told you not to bother me when I'm busy!" (The verb damn means to condemn to Hell, or eternal punishment after death. Christian church teachings forbid the use of this word as an expression of anger.)

damned; damn (dæmd, dæm) adj. vulgar. Annoying, broken, useless, worthless. "This *damned* car isn't any *damn* good!" "You *damned* idiot! You've ruined everything!"

***dark meat** ('dɑːrk miːt) vulgar expression. Sex with a black person. "Harry's buddies teased him about his black girlfriend. They asked him how he liked *dark meat*."

darn, darn it! (dɑːrn, dɑːrn ɪt) slang. interjections. Euphemisms for *damn* and *damn it*.

date rape ('deit reip) noun. slang. Forcible sexual intercourse while on a date. This is a crime.

***debut** (dei 'byuː) noun. slang. A gay person's first sexual experience with another gay person.

***deceive** (one's sex partner) (də 'siːv) verb. euphemism and general use. To hurt one's husband or wife (boyfriend or girlfriend) by having sexual relations with another person.

defecate ('dɛ fə keit) verb. formal. To expel (push out) feces from the rectum.

delicate parts of the anatomy ('dɛ lə kət pɑːrts əv ði ə 'næt ə mi) noun phrase, plural. euphemism. Genitals, usually male testicles. "Women, if you are attacked by a rapist," said the police officer, "kick him in the *delicate parts of his anatomy*."

derriere (dɛər iː 'ɛər) noun. euphemism. Buttocks. This word is borrowed from the French.

***desire** (də 'zaɪr) 1. verb. general use. To want in a sexual way. To have a sexual need for someone. 2. noun. general use. A sexual need. "His *desire* for her increased each day that she rejected him."

***dethroned** (diː 'θround) verb, past participle. gay slang. Caught by the police and sent out of a public toilet.

devil's dick ('dɛ vəlz 'dɪk) noun. vulgar. A pipe for smoking drugs.

***diaphragm** ('daɪ ə 'fræm) noun. formal and general use. A contraceptive device. It is a circular piece of rubber that is inserted into the woman's vagina before intercourse. It prevents sperm from entering the uterus. (There are many non-sexual uses of the word diaphragm, in the fields of anatomy, electronics, optics, and mechanics.)

diarrhea ('daɪ ə 'riː ə) noun. formal and general use. A need to defecate frequently. The feces are watery and hard to control. "Lynn had *diarrhea* from eating green apples." "The druggist said to take this medication to stop the baby's *diarrhea*."

dick (dɪk) noun. vulgar. The penis.

diddle ('dɪ dəl) verb. vulgar. 1. To masturbate. 2. To have sexual intercourse. 3. To waste time. "Stop *diddling* around, and get to work!" 4. To cheat someone.

*__dig out__ (dɪg 'aʊt) verb phrase. vulgar. Have sexual intercourse (from a male point of view).

dildo ('dɪl dou) noun. vulgar. 1. An artificial penis used for masturbation or sexual play. 2. An extremely stupid or clumsy person.

dingle berry ('dɪŋ gəl bɛr i) noun. vulgar. 1. A small piece of feces caught in the crotch hairs near the anus. 2. A stupid person.

*__dipstick__ ('dɪp stɪk) noun. vulgar. Penis. (A dipstick is a long measuring rod that is kept in a tube in a car's engine to check the level of oil in the car.

*__dirty__ ('dər ti) adj. slang. Having a vulgar or sexual meaning: dirty words, dirty pictures, dirty jokes, dirty movies, etc.

to have a dirty mind (tə hæv ə 'dər ti 'maɪnd) idiom. slang. To think of sex often. To think that other people are always thinking of sex. To interpret words with double meanings according to their sexual meanings rather than in their general-use meanings.

dirty old man noun. slang. An older man who is interested in flirting, touching, and seducing women. This may be used as a term of affection, or in a derogatory way.

*__discharge__ ('dɪs tʃaːrdʒ) noun. formal and general use. A liquid that comes out of the penis or vagina which may indicate that there is an infection or diseased condition. 'She went to the gynecologist for a check up because she had a frequent bad-smelling *discharge*." "One symptom of gonorrhea is a pus-like *discharge* from the penis."

*__diving suit__ ('daɪ vɪŋ suːt) noun. slang. Condom.

*__do it__ ('duː ɪt) verb. slang. To have sexual intercourse.

* words with additional meanings not listed

dog style ('dɔːg staɪ əl) adverb. slang. Sexual intercourse with the woman on her hands and knees, and the man entering the vagina from the rear.

***doodle** ('duː dəl) noun. vulgar. Penis.

doo doo ('duː 'duː) noun. children's word. Feces. Also: **doodee, make doo doo, defecate**.

dork (dɔːrk) noun. vulgar. Penis.

double meaning (dʌ bəl 'miː niŋ) noun. general use. Having two meanings, one of which is vulgar or sexual. "Words with *double meanings* are often the basis of jokes."

douche (duːʃ) verb. formal. To clean the vagina with water or medicated fluid, using a douche bag and syringe. "The doctor advised her to *douche* twice a week for four weeks." *Warning*: This word does not mean "shower." The Spanish word "ducha," French "douche," and other European words look similar, but the meanings are *not* the same.

douche bag ('duːʃ bæg) noun. general use. 1. The bag that contains the water for the douche. 2. vulgar. A very stupid and disliked person.

(go) down on (gou 'daʊn ɑn) verb. vulgar. To perform fellatio or cunnilingus. To give mouth-to-genital stimulation.

down there ('daʊn ðɛər) noun. euphemism. The pubic area. The genitals. "Tom fell off his bicycle and hurt himself, uh, you know...*down there*."

***drag** (dræg) noun. slang. A male who is wearing woman's clothing is said to be "in drag."

drain a lizard ('drein ə 'lɪ zərd) verb phrase. slang. Urinate.

drain a vein ('drein ə 'vein) verb phrase. slang. Urinate.

***drawers** (drɔːrz) noun. general use. Undershorts or panties.

drop one's load (drɑp wʌnz 'loud) verb phrase. vulgar. To ejaculate.

drop one's beads; drop one's hairpins (drɔp wʌnz biːds; drɔp wʌnz hɛər pɪnz) verb phrases. slang. To show through behavior that one is gay.

dry hump (draɪ hʌmp) verb. vulgar. To go through the motions of sexual intercourse completely clothed and without any actual genital contact.

duff (dʌf) noun. euphemism. The buttocks. "On one's duff" means *sitting*. "Get *off your duff* and let's get going."

***dump; dump a load** (dʌmp, dʌmp ə loud) verb phrase. vulgar. Defecate.

dung (dʌŋ) noun. 1. general use. Cow or horse droppings, manure. 2. slang. A hated person.

***duster** ('dʌ stər) noun. slang euphemism. The buttocks.

***dyke** (daɪk) noun. slang. A lesbian (female homosexual) who plays a masculine role. She may dress in mannish clothing, and walk, talk, and act in a masculine manner. A **diesel dyke** ('diː səl daɪk) is a large, very aggressive lesbian.

dysmenorrhea (dɪs 'mɛ nə ri ə) noun. formal and medical use. Painful cramps that accompany the menstrual period. "Some teenagers suffer from *dysmenorrhea*, but it is less common among mature women."

E

easy make (iː zi 'meik) noun. slang. A woman who will consent to have sexual intercourse with a man whom she doesn't know very well. Derogatory use.

***eat** (iːt) verb. vulgar. To perform cunnilingus or fellatio. To stimulate the genitals of one's partner with the mouth and tongue.

eat it raw verb phrase. vulgar. Cunnilingus

***egg** (ɛg) noun. general use. The ovum, or female sex cell.

*__ejaculate__ (ɪ ˈdʒæ kyə leit) verb. formal. Have a sexual orgasm, excreting semen.

*__eliminate__ (ə ˈlɪm ə neit) verb. formal. To excrete waste products. Technically, this word includes *perspiration*, *urination*, and *defecation*. It is often used, however, in the sense of *defecation* alone.

empty one's bladder (ˈɛmp ti wʌnz ˈblæ dər) verb phrase. formal. To urinate. Nurse to patient: "The doctor would like you to *empty your bladder* before the examination."

enema (ˈɛ nə mə) noun. general use. A cleaning-out of the rectum and lower colon by injecting warm water through the anus. "T. was constipated; the doctor advised him to take an *enema*." "The nurse gave the patient an *enema* before the operation."

enuresis (ɛ nyə ˈriː sɪs) noun. formal and medical use. 1. A problem of urinating in bed while one is asleep. "David suffered from *enuresis* until he was eleven years old." 2. Loss of control of the bladder. "Many elderly people begin to suffer from *enuresis*."

*__equipment__ (iː ˈkwɪp mənt) noun. slang. Male sex organs. **The right equipment** slang. **Well-equipped** adjective. slang. Having a large penis and testicles.

*__erect, to be__ (tə biː ə ˈrɛkt) verb phrase. general use. When the penis is firm, engorged with blood and ready for sexual intercourse.

*__erection__ (ə ˈrɛk ʃən) noun. general use. A firm or erect penis. "Ted gets an erection whenever he sees Connie." "Warren lost his *erection* when he heard the baby cry."

erotic (ə ˈra tɪk) adj. general use. Sexually stimulating. "Mike likes *erotic* stories and movies."

erotica (ə ˈra tɪ kə) noun, plural. general use. Collections of pictures and stories referring to sex.

***escort service** ('ɛs kɔːrt 'sər vɪs) noun. euphemism. A business that provides male or female companions to accompany a person to a party, event, or gathering, for a fee. It often includes sexual favors.

eunuch ('yu nək) noun. formal and general use. A male whose testicles have been removed in childhood, or whose testicles do not function normally. A *eunuch* does not have a deep masculine voice, beard, or pubic hair, and cannot have sexual intercourse.

***excited** (ɛk 'saɪ təd) adj. general use. Aroused sexually. "X-rated videos get Dan *excited.*"

***exhibitionist** (ɛk sɪ 'bɪ ʃə nɪst) noun. general use. 1. A person who acts in a way to attract attention to himself. Actors, politicians, and other performers are exhibitionists in a way. 2. A person who receives sexual pleasure from showing parts of his or her body in public to strangers.

***expect** (ɪk 'spekt) verb. general use. To wait for the birth of a baby. To be pregnant. "Judy is *expecting* in July." (She will give birth to a baby in July.)

expectant (ɪk 'spek tant) adj. general use. Pregnant. "Mrs. Thomas went to a clinic for *expectant* mothers." "When are you *expecting*?" is a common question asked of pregnant women. "The Johnsons are *expecting* a visit from the stork." (A stork is a large bird with a very long bill. A few generations ago, parents did not feel comfortable in discussing reproduction with children, so they told them that babies are "brought by the stork.")

F

F (ɛf) verb. vulgar euphemism. Abbreviation of fuck. "*F you!*" she shouted." "Get *the F* out of here!" "Where's the *F-ing* key?"

***facilities** (fə 'sɪl ə tiːs) noun, plural. slang. The bathroom. "Excuse me, may I use your *facilities*?"

* words with additional meanings not listed

facts of life ('fækts əv laɪf) noun phrase. euphemism. The facts about sex and reproduction. "H. thought his son was old enough to learn *the facts of life*. It was too late. His son had learned them from a friend when the kids were six years old."

fag; faggot (fæg, 'fæ gət) noun. derogatory slang. A male homosexual.

***fairy** ('fɛər i) noun. slang. A homosexual.

***faithful** ('feiθ fəl) adj. general use, euphemism. Having sexual intercourse with one partner only. "M.'s husband has always been *faithful* to her, and she has been a *faithful* wife." **unfaithful**. (ʌn 'feiθ fəl) adj. euphemism. The *opposite* of faithful. "When Gina found out her husband had been *unfaithful*, she was miserable."

fake an orgasm; fake it ('feik ən 'ɔːr gæ zəm; 'feik ɪt) verb phrase. slang. To pretend to reach a sexual climax by dramatically acting as if one were receiving intense pleasure. "Marcia *faked* her orgasms to please her husband."

falsies ('fɔl siːz) noun, plural. slang. Rubber or cotton pads placed in a woman's brassiere to give the appearance of having larger breasts. "Nobody knew she wore *falsies*."

family jewels ('fæm ə li 'dzu wəlz) noun, plural. slang, humorous. The male sex organs, *penis* and *testicles*. (Jewels are precious stones, such as rubies and diamonds. This expression shows a high regard placed on the male sex organs.)

fanny ('fæ ni) noun. slang. The buttocks.

fan one's ass; fan one's pussy (fæn wʌnz æs, fæn wʌnz pʊ si) verb phrase. vulgar. (For a woman) Dress and walk in a way that shows off one's sexual attractiveness.

fart (fɑːrt) 1. verb. vulgar. Expel gas from the rectum. "Beans make you *fart*." "Larry *farted* and blamed it on the dog." 2. noun. vulgar. The gas that is expelled. 3. verb phrases. vulgar. **lay a fart; blow a fart; let loose a fart; give out a fart.** Expel gas.

feces (fiː siːz) noun, plural. formal and medical use. The undigested waste that is expelled from the rectum when one goes to the toilet.

fellatio (fɛ lei ʃiː ou) noun. formal. Oral-genital contact. Mouth-to-penis sexual stimulation.

perform fellatio formal. To give sexual pleasure by stimulating the penis with the mouth.

feminine syringe ('fɛ mɪ nɪn sə 'rɪndʒ) noun. euphemism. A douche bag and hose for cleaning the vagina.

fetishist ('fɛt ɪ ʃɪst) noun. formal. A person who becomes sexually aroused by a particular part of a person, clothing, or some object. "She was a hair *fetishist*, and he was a foot *fetishist*. With her pretty feet, and his mop of hair, they got along very well."

*__flasher__ ('flæʃ ər) noun. slang. A man who gets sexually aroused by showing his penis to female strangers in public. He may wear a raincoat covering his unzippered pants, and flash his coat open when a woman alone approaches him.

flog one's dong (flɑg wʌnz dɔŋ) verb phrase. vulgar. Masturbate.

*__fly__ (flaɪ) noun. general use. The zipper or buttons in the front of trousers or pants. "J. was embarrassed to discover that his *fly* was open. He quickly zipped it up."

forbidden fruit (fər bɪ dən 'fruːt) noun phrase. slang. A person who is under the age of consent. This age is set by law in each state. Sex between an older person and an underage person is rape, with a serious punishment. (Often twenty years in jail.)

***foreplay** ('fɔːr plei) noun. general use. Sexual play before intercourse. Includes touching, kissing, talking, massaging, etc. "D. wanted her husband to pay more attention to *foreplay* when he made love to her."

foreskin ('fɔːr skɪn) noun. formal. The skin that covers the penis when it is not erect.

fornicate ('fɔːr nə keit) verb. formal and legal use and derogatory general use. To have sexual intercourse with someone to whom one is not married. "*Fornication* is against the law in many states."

foul language (faʊl 'læŋ gwɪdʒ) noun. general use. Vulgar language. "We don't want any *foul language* in this playground," said the police officer.

foul mouth (faʊl maʊθ) noun. general use. A person who uses vulgar words frequently in places where this is socially unacceptable. "My friend Gert has a *foul mouth*. I'm embarrassed to go to parties with her."

four-letter words ('fɔːr lɛt ər wʌrdʒ) noun, plural. general use. Vulgar words. Many vulgar words contain just four letters. Some common ones are *piss*, *shit*, *fart*, *fuck*, *cock*, *cunt*, *hell*, *damn*.

***fox** (fɑks) also, **foxy lady** noun. slang. A sexually attractive, clever, independent, and fashionable woman. "Monica is quite a *fox*."

free love (friː lʌv) noun. 1. euphemism. Used by older people. Sexual relationships without marriage. "The younger generations all believe in *free love*," complained Harry's grandmother. "In my day, you waited until the minister tied the knot." 2. slang. Promiscuous sex without any emotional or moral bond between the partners.

***French** (frɛntʃ) verb. slang. To perform fellatio or cunnilingus. Oral stimulation of the genitals. Also, **speak French.**

French dressing (frɛntʃ 'drɛ sɪŋ) noun. slang. Semen. Homosexual use.

French kiss (frɛntʃ 'kɪs) noun. slang. Kissing in which one's tongue is inserted into the partner's mouth.

French letter (frɛntʃ 'lɛt ər) noun. slang. A condom.

fresh fruit (frɛʃ 'fru:t) noun. vulgar. very derogatory. A new arrival to a social group of homosexuals.

F

***friend** (frɛnd) noun. euphemism. The menstrual period. "I can't go swimming because I've got *my friend*."

frig (frɪg) verb. vulgar. euphemism for *fuck*. Generally used in expressions that do not imply sexual intercourse. **friggin'** (frɪg'n) less offensive form of *fucking* (as an adjective). "Where is that *friggin'* wallet?"

***frigid** ('frɪ dʒɪd) adj. general use. 1. Cold. 2. Unable to respond sexually. (Said of a woman.) Unable to have orgasm. "It is as miserable to be a *frigid* wife as it is to have a *frigid* wife."

frigidity (frɪ 'dʒɪ də ti) noun. general use. Inability to respond sexually. "C. went to a sex-therapy clinic to see if her *frigidity* could be cured."

***fruit** (fru:t) noun. slang. Homosexual. (derogatory)

fuck (fʌk) verb. vulgar. 1. To have sexual intercourse (with). This is the most common vulgar word for *sexual intercourse*. The word *fuck* also has many meanings that have no relationship with sexual activity. They are all considered vulgar. 2. To treat badly or unfairly; to cheat. "Don't deal with that company; they *fuck* all their customers." "J. got *fucked* by his business partners and lost all his money." 3. The words *the fuck* may be added in the middle of a command, to add emphasis or show anger: "Shut *the fuck* up!" "Sit *the fuck* down." It may be added to questions, with the same effect: "Who *the fuck* is that? Where *the fuck* are we? Why *the fuck* didn't you tell me? What *the fuck* are you doing?"

fuck around (fʌk ə 'raʊnd) verb. vulgar. 1. Fool around. Annoy. "Stop *fucking around*! I'm getting angry." 2. Be idle; loiter at a place without any purposeful activity. "We went down to the ball field and just *fucked around* for a while. There wasn't anything else to do."

fucker ('fʌ kər) noun. vulgar. 1. Disliked person. "Bob? Oh, that *fucker*? Don't trust him." 2. Unfortunate person. "A drunk tried to cross the street against the light. The poor *fucker* got hit by a car."

fucking ('fʌ kɪŋ)/('fʌ kɪn) adj. vulgar. 1. Bad, rotten, no-good, worthless. "P. is a *fucking* idiot." 2. Among some all-male groups, such as sailors, soldiers, members of sports teams, prisoners, construction workers, and others, the word *fucking* is used by habit as an adjective in front of any noun. "Pass the *fucking* salt." "Where's the *fucking* knife?" It has no meaning, other than to establish either the manhood of the speaker, or the bond among men of a similar social class. 3. adverb. vulgar. Very. "That's *fucking* great!" The word *fucking* is also used as an internal affix of a long word. Absolutely becomes *abso-fucking-lutely*. Unconscious becomes *un-fucking-conscious*. Irresponsible becomes *irre-fucking-sponsible*.

fuck off (fʌk ɑf) verb. vulgar. Go away; stop bothering someone. "I was too busy to listen to his complaints, so I told him to *fuck off*."

fuck one's fist verb phrase. vulgar. Masturbate.

fuck one's mind verb phrase. vulgar. Brainwash. To confuse permanently. "Ivan started using heroin and it really *fucked his mind*. He steals from his parents to pay for his drugs."

fuck up ('fʌk 'ʌp) verb. vulgar. Do an incompetent job, creating more work for others. Ruin; confuse; make serious errors. "The hospital really *fucked up* this bill." "The architect *fucked up* the design of the house. He didn't leave enough room for the upstairs stairway."

fuck-up ('fʌk ʌp) noun. vulgar. An incompetent person. Someone who usually makes things worse when he does a job. "D. is a real *fuck-up*. No matter how many times you explain something to him, he manages to do it wrong."

fucked up ('fʌkt 'ʌp) adjective. vulgar. Incorrectly assembled; broken in many places. "This engine is all *fucked up*." Drunk; stoned (on drugs); sad. "Al gets *fucked up* every weekend."

F

fuck someone up verb. vulgar. Cause someone to suffer mental or physical injury. To confuse. "The suicide *fucked him up* real bad."

fuck with ('fʌk wɪθ) verb. vulgar. Interfere with; touch with intention of hurting or damaging; deal with in a dishonest way. "Anyone who *fucks with* old Sam better be careful. Sam'll kill him."

fuck you! interjection. vulgar. 1. Damn you! Said in great anger with hopes that the listener will have serious bad luck. 2. No. Leave me alone. You irritate me.

(Go) fuck yourself! interjection. vulgar. Interjection showing great anger and contempt for the listener.

I don't give a fuck! expression. vulgar. I don't care in the least. It's completely unimportant to me. "*I don't give a fuck* what you say; I'm going to do this my way."

full of it; full of bull; full of crap phrases. euphemisms for **full of shit.** vulgar. Full of lies and exaggerated stories. "Don't listen to J. He's *full of it*."

***fundament** ('fʌn də mənt) noun. slang. The buttocks.

funky ('fʌn ki) adjective. slang. Having a bad body odor. "It was hot and sticky. The dancers got all *funky* by the end of the evening."

furburger ('fər bər gər) noun. vulgar. The vulva. The entrance to the vagina.

* words with additional meanings not listed

G

G-spot (dʒiː spɑt) noun. slang. A small area in the front wall of the vagina that, when stimulated during intercourse or masturbation, causes female ejaculation and a great release of body tension.

gang bang ('gæŋ bæŋ) noun. vulgar. 1. An event during which several males take turns having intercourse with one female. This act may be considered group rape, or have the female's consent. 2. Sex in a group.

***gas** (gæs) noun. general use. Intestinal gas. "Doctor, I get *gas* when I eat cabbage."

pass gas (pæs 'gæs) verb. general use. Expel gas from the rectum.

***gay** (gei) adj. slang. Homosexual, either male or female. This word is preferred by homosexuals. It is non-derogatory. In the past few years, Americans have stopped using the word *gay* in its former meaning of "happy, jolly, care-free," in order to avoid misunderstanding. An older person might still say, "It was a *gay* party." However, to most Americans, this sentence now means "It was a party for homosexuals," and not, "It was a jolly party."

Gay Rights Movement (gei raɪts 'muːv mənt) noun. general use. Organized campaigns, demonstrations, and activities to increase the rights of homosexuals. Also referred to as Gay Liberation or Gay Activism. Some of the goals are: change laws that discriminate against homosexuals; gain equal rights in employment, housing, health care, and child custody laws.

gaydar ('gei dɑːr) noun. slang. The extra "sense" that a gay person has that tells him or her if another person is gay or not.

gender ('dʒɛn dər) noun. general use. There are 3 genders: masculine (male), feminine (female), and neuter (neither male nor female). "What *gender* are the puppies?" "They're *male*." "We had our male cat *neutered*."

genitalia (dʒɛ nə 'tei li ə) noun, plural. formal. Sex organs. Reproductive organs of male or female. "The penis and testicles, and vagina and vulva all are parts of *human genitalia.*"

*__get hot__ (gɛt 'hɑt) verb phrase. slang. Become sexually excited.

get into her pants verb phrase. vulgar. Have sexual intercourse with a woman. "Vic wanted to *get into his girlfriend's pants*, but she was waiting for an engagement ring."

get one's end wet verb phrase. vulgar. Be successful at seducing a woman. "*Get your end wet* last night?" his roommate asked.

get it up (gɛt ɪt 'ʌp) verb phrase. slang. Have an erection. "Jack drank too much at the party. Although he felt romantic, he couldn't *get it up*."

get a little action (gɛt ə lɪt əl 'æk ʃən) noun. slang. Sexual activity. The sailors visited a bar to see if they could *get a little action* with the women there.

*__get off__ verb phrase. slang. Be sexually satisfied; ejaculate; have an orgasm. "Jay *gets off* on dirty movies."

get one's shit together verb phrase. vulgar. To get organized; become prepared. "It's just a few days before the inspectors come, and this place is a mess. We've got to *get our shit together*, and straighten up."

get to first base (gɛt tə fərst beis) verb phrase. slang. Be successful in getting a girl or woman's interest; get to touch a woman's breast on a date. (A baseball analogy of the steps to seduction. *Home run*, or *scoring*, is to have intercourse.) Usually in the negative. "I couldn't *get to first base* with her."

gigolo ('dʒɪ gə lou) noun. general use. A young man who has a relationship with a woman (usually older, or richer). He is not paid as a prostitute, but may receive money, gifts, presents, favors, or complete support in appreciation for his attention.

give head (gɪv ˈhɛd) verb phrase. vulgar. Perform fellatio, or cunnilingus. Give mouth-to-genital stimulation.

***give a shot** verb phrase. vulgar. Ejaculate in a woman.

gluteus maximus (ˈgluː tiː əs ˈmæk sɪ məs) noun. formal and medical use. The buttocks. The word is also used humorously. "Get off your *gluteus maximus* and start to work."

***go** (gou) verb. euphemism. Abbreviated form of go to the toilet. "Hurry up in the bathroom. I have to *go*!"

go down, go downtown verb. euphemism. Oral sex.

gonads (ˈgou nædz) noun, plural. formal and medical use. The reproductive organs; the testes and the ovaries. Sex glands. **nads** noun. slang. Gonads.

gonorrhea (gɑ nə ˈriː ə) noun. formal and medical use. A disease that affects the sex organs. It is acquired through sexual contact with someone who has it. One of the venereal diseases. Symptoms in the man are a pus-filled discharge from the penis, and painful urination. "A woman may have *gonorrhea* with no visible external symptoms."

goose (guːs) verb. slang. To quickly poke something, such as a finger, into another person's anus. This may be done as a joke or as playful teasing.

go up the old dirt road verb phrase. vulgar. Have anal sex.

Greek way (griːk wei) adverbial phrase. slang. Anal intercourse.

groin (grɔɪn) noun. general use. The crotch area. The pubic area. "The football player pulled a muscle in his *groin*."

gynecologist (gaɪ nə ˈkɑ lə dʒəst) noun. formal. A doctor who specializes in treating women's reproductive organs. A gynecologist may also be an **obstetrician** (ɑb stə ˈtrɪ ʃən), a specialist in delivering babies.

H

hair pie (hɛər paɪ) noun. vulgar. The female genitalia, especially when considered as the object of cunnilingus, or mouth-to-genital stimulation.

half-assed (hæf æst) adj. vulgar. Stupid, lazy.

half-and-half (hæf ən hæf) adj. slang. Bisexual.

***hams** (hæmz) noun, plural. slang. The buttocks.

***hammer** ('hæm ər) noun. vulgar. The penis. "Hey Joe, what's new? How's your *hammer* hanging?" (A greeting between males.)

hand job ('hænd dʒɑb) noun phrase. slang. Masturbation by hand.

hard on ('hɑːrd ɑn) noun. vulgar. An erection (of the penis). "Gary wakes up every morning with a *hard on.*"

harlot ('hɑːr lət) noun. slang. A cheap prostitute.

***head** (hɛd) noun. 1. slang. The bathroom. This term is most common among sailors, but is also used in bars and taverns. 2. general use. The head of the penis.

to give head (tə gɪv 'hɛd) verb phrase. vulgar. To perform fellatio or cunnilingus on one's partner. To orally stimulate the genitals.

***to have a headache** (tə hæv ə 'hɛd eik) verb phrase. euphemism. Often said by a person when he or she is not interested in having sex at the moment. "Not tonight, honey–I've got a headache" is now a standard joke.

***headlights** ('hɛd laɪts) noun, plural. vulgar. A woman's breasts, especially large ones.

***heat,** bitch in (hiːt) noun. vulgar. A sexually aggressive woman.

heinie ('haɪ ni) noun. children's word. The buttocks.

***helmet** ('hɛl mɛt) noun. slang. 1. A condom. 2. The head of the penis.

* words with additional meanings not listed

Hell (hɛl) noun. general use. Hell is a place where the souls or spirits of dead people go if they had been bad during their life on earth (according to traditional Christian teachings). In Hell, the souls are punished by fire and by devils. The opposite of Heaven. The use of this word is restricted by church teachings. It is considered "swearing" when used in anger. However, it is very common.

Go to Hell! (gou tə hɛl) Expression. Mild blasphemy. Interjection of annoyance at someone.

the hell noun. blasphemy. The words "the hell" add emphasis and anger to the question that follows. Why *the hell* did you do that? What *the hell* do you think you're doing? Where *the hell* are you going? Who *the hell* do you think you are? Not approved for polite society.

***hemispheres** ('hɛ mɪs fiərz) noun, plural. slang. A woman's breasts.

hemorrhoids ('hɛ mə rɔɪdz) noun. formal and general use. Painful enlargements of veins near the anus. **Piles.** "His doctor told him that chronic constipation can cause *hemorrhoids.*"

hermaphrodite (hər 'mæ frə daɪt) noun. formal. A person who was born with both male and female sex organs.

herpes ('hər piːz) noun. formal and general use. There is oral (on the mouth) herpes and genital herpes. It is a virus that causes painful blisters. It can be transmitted through kissing, sex, toilet seats, and sharing the same drinking glass or towels.

Hershey Highway ('hər ʃiː 'haɪ wei) noun phrase. slang. The rectum, when used for anal intercourse. Hershey comes from the name of a famous chocolate candy bar.

Hershey squirts ('hər ʃiː skwərts) noun phrase, plural. Diarrhea. Frequent and watery bowel movements.

heterosexual (hɛt ə rou 'sɛk ʃuː əl) noun and adj. formal and general use. Someone who prefers sexual relations with a member of the opposite sex. The opposite of homosexual (attracted to the same sex as oneself).

***Hi...** (haɪː) A greeting. When drawled slowly, with a gentle smile, homosexuals often can identify each other by the tone of voice without needing to say anything else.

hickey ('hɪ ki) noun. slang. A purple or reddish mark that results from passionate nibbling or sucking on the skin, usually in the neck, shoulder, and chest areas.

***high beams on** (haɪ biːmz ɑn) adverbial phrase. slang. When a woman's nipples are erect and noticeable through her clothing. "Take a look at that one. She's got her *high beams on.*"

H

hind end (haɪnd ɛnd) noun. euphemism. The buttocks.

***hold it** (hould ɪt) verb phrase. general use. To control one's need to have a bowel movement or to urinate. "I can't *hold it* till we get home. Could you stop at a gas station so I can use the rest room?"

***hole** (houl) noun. vulgar. The vagina.

homo ('hou mou) noun. slang. derogatory use. A homosexual.

homosexual ('hou mou 'sɛk ʃuː əl) noun and adjective. formal and general use. Any person, male or female, who prefers sexual relations with persons of the same sex.

***honey pot** ('hʌ niː pɑt) noun. slang. A woman's genitals.

***hooker** ('hʊ kər) noun. slang. A prostitute. "You can walk down Eighth Avenue near 42nd Street and see all the *hookers* waiting for customers.

hooters ('huːt ərz) noun, plural. vulgar. Breasts.

***horn** noun. slang. Penis.

***horny** ('hɔːr ni) adj. slang. Desiring sexual activity. "The sailors were all *horny* after six weeks at sea."

***hot** (hɑt) adj. slang. Aroused sexually. "She was *hot* and breathing hard." "I'm so *hot* for you," he whispered.

* words with additional meanings not listed

hot flashes (hɑt ˈflæ ʃəz) noun, plural. general use. A symptom that sometimes accompanies the menopause in middle-aged women. The whole body may suddenly feel a quick flash of heat. "B. complained to her doctor about the *hot flashes* she was having."

hot and heavy (ˈhɑt ən ˈhɛ vi) adverbs. slang. With sexual excitement. "He was breathing all *hot and heavy*."

hot number (hɑt ˈnʌm bər) noun. slang. A cute and sexy person. Jack told Fred that he had met a real *hot number* at the party.

hot shit (ˈhɑt ˈʃɪt) noun. vulgar. Important person. Used in a derogatory sense. "Frank thinks he's *hot shit*, but in my opinion he's a big zero."

hot to trot (hɑt tə trɑt) adj. slang. Ready for sexual activity.

*__hump__ (hʌmp) verb. vulgar. Have sexual intercourse with.

*__hung; hung like a mule__ (hʌŋ, hʌŋ laɪk ə ˈmyul) adj. vulgar. To have a penis and testicles the size of a mule's. (A mule is a large animal much like a horse.) "Donald is *hung like a mule*." "Val is really *hung*." (He has very large genitals.) Chet is *hung like a mouse*. (He has small genitals.)

*__hustler__ (ˈhʌs lər) noun. slang. A prostitute.

hymen (ˈhaɪ mən) noun. formal. The membrane (skin) that partly covers the vagina before a woman's first sexual intercourse. An unbroken hymen is considered to be a sign of virginity. This is not as important in American society as it was two generations ago. Today, when young women abstain from sex it is rarely to preserve their virginity. In most cases it is to avoid sexually transmitted diseases.

hysterectomy (hɪ stə ˈrɛk tə mi) noun. formal. A surgical operation to remove the uterus.

illegitimate (ɪ lə 'dʒɪ tə mət) adjective. formal and legal use (derogatory). Not legal; not within marriage. This term is no longer politically correct: *all* children have a legitimate right to be here. The evidence for that is: they *are* here.

***impotent** ('ɪm pə tənt) adj. formal and general use. Unable to get or keep an erection long enough to have successful sexual intercourse.

impotence ('ɪm pə təns) noun. formal. The inability to have sexual intercourse. "Glen hoped an improved diet would help his *impotence*."

impregnate (ɪm 'prɛg neit) verb. formal. To make a female pregnant. "A single man is capable of *impregnating* thousands of women."

incest ('ɪn sɛst) noun. formal and general use. Incest is a sexual relationship between people who are so closely related that they would not be allowed to marry. The law forbids marriage between brother and sister, first cousins, parent and child, grandparent and child, uncle or aunt and child.

incontinent (ɪn 'kɑn tɪ nənt) adj. formal and medical use. Unable to stop the flow of urine from the bladder. "The elderly woman was embarrassed because she was *incontinent* and often passed urine when she laughed or sneezed." This term may also refer to inability to control defecation.

infertility (ɪn fər 'tɪ lə ti) noun. formal. Inability to have children. "After four years of marriage with no children, Don and his wife went to an *infertility* clinic to get medical help."

infidelity (ɪn fə 'dɛ lə ti) noun. general use. Unfaithfulness. Sex with a partner who is not one's own husband or wife. "Hal accused his wife of *infidelity* when he found out she had been seeing an old boyfriend."

***innocent** ('ɪ nə sənt) adj. euphemism. Inexperienced sexually. "Hillary was *innocent* until she was nineteen years old."

***intercourse** ('ɪn tər kɔːrs) noun. formal and general use. 1. Human or business relations or communications. 2. Sexual intercourse. "Some newly married couples have *intercourse* twice or more a day."

***intimate** ('ɪn tə mət) adj. 1. general use. Emotionally or physically close. "Lorna is my *intimate* friend." 2. euphemism. Sexually intimate. "Brian and Rita were *intimate* before they were married."

***irregular** (ɪ 'rɛg yu lər) adj. euphemism. 1. Constipated; have difficulties in defecation. Not having regular bowel movements. "Olivia takes hot water and lemon juice in the morning whenever she is *irregular*." 2. Having irregular menstrual periods.

***it** (ɪt) noun. slang. euphemism. 1. Sex appeal. "Leo has *it*." 2. The male sex organ. The penis. 3. The female sex organs. The vagina. 4. **do it; make it; make it with** = have sexual intercourse.

***itch** (ɪtʃ) noun. slang. The desire for sexual experience. **the seven-year itch** noun. slang. A married man is said to be satisfied with his own wife for the first seven years of marriage, and then begins to look around at other women, and "*itch*" to have relations with them. "Fred has *the seven-year itch* and he's only been married two years!"

I.U.D. (aɪː yuː diː) noun. formal and medical use. An intra-uterine device (ɪn trə 'yu də rɪn də 'vaɪs). A method of birth control. The device is a specially shaped plastic and metal loop which is permanently inserted into a woman's uterus by a doctor. It prevents pregnancy.

J

jack off (dʒæk ɔːf) verb. vulgar. Masturbate.

jail bait (dʒeil beit) noun. slang. A person under the legal "age of consent" (which is different in each state). If a person over the legal age has sexual intercourse with a girl or boy under the age, he or she may be accused of rape. This may happen even if the young person was a willing partner. This is called **statutory rape** ('stæ tʃyu tʊə ri reip). The punishment is up to twenty years in jail.

jazz around (dʒæz ə 'raʊnd) verb phrase. slang. Have intercourse.

jerk off (dʒərk ɔːf) verb. vulgar. Masturbate.

Jesus ('dʒiː zəs) noun. restricted use. In the Christian religion, *Jesus* is the name of the Son of God. This name may be used in any informative discussion of *Jesus* or His teachings, but it is considered blasphemy among Christians to use it in a disrespectful manner. However, it is heard quite frequently.

Jesus Christ (dʒiː zəs 'kraɪst) noun. restricted use. According to Christian teachings, the divine human appointed by God to be the Savior. The Christian church forbids the use of the name in disrespectful ways.

Jesus, **Jesus Christ**, and **Christ** are often used in expressions of surprise, anger, or pain. (This is done in spite of the church's restrictions.)

Jesus-freak ('dʒiː zəs friːk) noun. slang, offensive. A person who has joined a sect of Christianity that requires him or her to leave their home, collect money from the public, and try to convert others.

jew down (dzuː 'daʊn) verb. vulgar. Derogatory to Jews. To argue with a salesman over a price, trying to get something for less money.

jism ('dʒɪ zəm) noun. slang. Semen. Also *gism*, *jizz*.

jock itch ('dʒɑk ɪtʃ) noun. slang. An itchy rash in the crotch area between the legs. It may be caused by heavy sweating.

jockstrap ('dʒɑk stræp) noun. slang. An athletic supporter. A garment worn by males to support the genitals and protect them from injury during athletic activities, games, sports, etc.

***john** (dʒɑn) noun. slang. The bathroom.

Johnson (dʒɑn sən) noun. slang. The penis.

***joint** (dʒɔɪnt) noun. vulgar. The penis.

***joystick** ('dʒɔɪ stɪk) noun. vulgar. The penis.

***jugs** (dʒʌgz) noun, plural. slang. A woman's breasts.

K

ka ka ('kɑ kɑ) noun. children's word. Feces. **make ka ka.** verb phrase. Defecate.

keester ('kiː stər) noun. slang. The buttocks.

***kinky** ('kɪŋ ki) adj. slang. 1. Unusual, experimental, strange, as in *kinky sex*. "George always dressed like a woman to make love to his wife. That seemed *kinky* to her. She enjoyed being tied to the bed, which seemed *kinky* to George." 2. Homosexual.

kiss my ass! (kɪs maɪː æs) vulgar expression: No, I certainly *won't* do what you asked. "Hank asked me to lend him money again, and I told him to *kiss my ass*."

***knob** (nɑb) noun. slang. Penis.

***knockers** ('nɑ kərz) noun, plural. vulgar. A woman's breasts.

knock up (nɑk 'ʌp) verb. vulgar. To get a woman pregnant. "Jay *knocked up* his girlfriend and was afraid his wife would find out."

to get knocked up (tə gɛt nɑkt 'ʌp) verb phrase. vulgar. To become pregnant. "Corey's daughter *got knocked up*, so Corey forced Thomas to marry her."

***know** (nou) verb. euphemism, very old-fashioned use. Have sexual intercourse with. This is the term used in the Christian Bible. "And Adam *knew* his wife and she brought forth Cain." It is now used as a euphemism, jokingly. A: "I *knew* Sally in school." B: "In the Biblical sense?" A: "No, just as classmates."

L

labia ('lei biː ə) noun. formal and medical use. The folds of flesh around the vagina.

lady of easy virtue ('lei di əv 'iː ziː 'vər tʃyuː) noun. euphemism. A prostitute.

lady of the night ('lei di əv ðə naɪt) noun. euphemism. A prostitute.

latrine (lə 'triːn) noun. general use. A hole dug into the ground for use as a toilet; a toilet.

lavatory ('læ və tɔ ri) noun. euphemism. Toilet. (This word comes from the French and means *washroom*. Do not confuse with *laboratory*, a place where scientists work.)

***lay** (lei) 1. verb. vulgar. Have sexual intercourse. "He *laid* her twice." "She wanted to get *laid*." 2. noun. vulgar. The quality of a woman as a sexual partner. "Cassandra looked like a good *lay* to him." "To be a good *lay*, a woman should have a nice body and a passionate nature," he said.

laxative ('læk sə tɪv) noun. general use. A food or medicine that causes or promotes a bowel movement. "Dried fruit such as prunes act as a *laxative* for most people." "Katrina was constipated, so she used a *laxative* that her doctor recommended."

lead in one's pencil ('lɛd ɪn wʌnz 'pɛn səl) noun phrase. slang. The ability to get and keep a firm erection. "I hear that eating oysters puts *lead in your pencil*."

lecher ('lɛ tʃər) noun. general use, derogatory. A person who has strong sexual desires. This word implies that the person is immoral (already married) or vulgar in his attentions to the persons he leches after.

lechery ('lɛ tʃə ri) noun. general use. Excessive (too much) sexual interest or activity. "A very proper and strictly religious person might think that there is too much *lechery* in the world today."

lecherous ('lɛ tʃə rɛs) adj. general use. Having strong sexual desires. This word is used by someone who is not interested in the attention of such a person. "Justin is a *lecherous* old fool," said Marla.

lesbian ('lɛz biː ən) noun. formal and general use. A female homosexual.

lewd (luːd) adj. general use. Lustful. Interested in sex.

*__library__ ('laɪ brɛr i) noun. slang. The bathroom. (So named because many people read in the bathroom, and keep books and magazines there.)

*__lie with__ ('laiː wɪθ) verb phrase. euphemism. Have sexual intercourse with.

in the life (ɪn ðə 'laɪf) noun phrase. euphemism. 1. Working as a prostitute. 2. Living in the culture of homosexuals and lesbians.

little black book ('lɪt əl blæk 'bʊk) noun. slang. A man's address book containing the names and phone numbers of the sex partners he has had, or would like to have–and sometimes with comments about them.

live in sin (lɪv ɪn 'sɪn) verb phrase. derogatory euphemism for *fornicate*. To live as man and wife in the same home without being married to each other. According to religious teachings, this is a sin, a crime against God's laws. "Mrs. Jameson refused to visit her daughter because she felt that the girl was *living in sin* with a boyfriend."

*__live together__ (lɪv tə gɛ 'ðɛr) verb phrase. euphemism. To live as husband and wife in the same home without being married to each other. No derogatory judgment is implied in this word. "Rick and Tanya *lived together* for three years before they got married."

*__loins__ (lɔɪnz) noun, plural. euphemism. The reproductive organs. The crotch area.

*__loose__ (luːs) adjective. euphemism. Promiscuous. Having many sex partners, or not being careful in the choice of sexual partners.

*__lungs__ (lʌŋz) noun, plural. slang. A woman's breasts. (among men) Only a man would ask someone, "Did you see the pair of *lungs* on that singer?"

*__lust__ (lʌst) 1. verb. general use. To have sexual desire. "Jose lusts after all big-breasted women." 2. noun. general use. strong sexual desire. "Sexy movies are made to arouse lust."

M

M

*__madam__ ('mæ dəm) noun. general use. A woman who manages a house of prostitution.

__maidenhead__ ('mei dən hɛd) noun. euphemism. The hymen, a flap of skin that partly covers the vagina before a woman has her first sexual experience.

*__make__ (meik) verb. slang. Have sexual intercourse with. "Frank has *made* 75% of all the girls he's dated." "I can be *made*," she said.

__make it with__ (meik ɪt wɪθ) verb phrase. slang. Have a successful relationship, including sexual relations. "Bill would like to *make it with* Susie, but she doesn't seem to care for him."

__make love__ (meik 'lʌv) verb phrase. euphemism. Have sexual intercourse (with). This expression implies tenderness and affectionate emotion, besides the simple physical act. "Marcie and Tom had a beautiful evening: First they ate at a fine restaurant, then they saw a good movie, and finally they went home and *made love*."

__make out__ (with) (meik 'aʊt) verb phrase. slang. Spend time hugging, kissing, and petting (touching). "When we were teenagers, we used to *make out* in drive-in movies."

* words with additional meanings not listed

make-out artist ('meik aʊt 'ɑːr təst) noun. slang. A person who enjoys making out, possibly with a different girl on each occasion. "Is this your first date with Gary? Be careful–he's known as a real *make-out artist*."

make a rude noise (meik ə ruːd nɔɪz) verb phrase. euphemism. Pass gas.

mammary glands ('mæ mə ri glændz) noun, plural. formal and medical use. The breasts. The glands that produce milk for newborn babies. "All mammals have **mammary glands** to produce milk for their young."

man in the boat (mæn ɪn ðə 'bout) noun phrase. slang. Clitoris.

maricon (mɑ riː 'koun) noun. vulgar, derogatory. Homosexual. (From the Spanish.)

masochism ('mæ sə kɪ zəm) noun. formal and general use. A perversion in which a person (a *masochist*) receives pleasure from pain, insult or being badly treated. "A *masochist* may want his sex partner to tie him with ropes and beat him with a leather strap."

***massage parlor** (mə 'sɑʒ 'pɑːr lər) noun. euphemism. House of prostitution.

masturbate ('mæ stər beit) verb. formal and general use. To touch and stimulate one's own genitals in order to have an orgasm. **masturbation** (mæ stər 'bei ʃən) noun form.

***mate** (meit) noun. general use. 1. A sexual partner; a husband or wife. A more-or-less permanent lover and companion. A man may refer to his wife as his "mate." This implies an affectionate feeling toward her. "Thanks for the dinner invitation; I'll let you know if we can come as soon as I talk with my *mate*." 2. An animal's sexual partner in producing young ones. "It's *mating* season; all the male deer are looking for *mates*." 3. verb. general use. To copulate for the purposes of producing babies or young ones, as animals do. "Brenda's purebred Siamese cat ran out of the house and *mated* with an ugly old alley cat."

***meat** (miːt) noun. vulgar. The penis.

beat the meat (biːt ðə miːt) verb phrase. vulgar. Masturbate.

meat house (miːt haʊs) noun. vulgar. House of prostitution.

***member** ('mɛm bər) noun. euphemism. The penis.

ménàge à trois (mə 'nɑʒ ɑ 'trwɑ) noun. slang. Three partners having sexual intercourse. "Ben invited his girlfriend and her roommate on a date. It was his fantasy to have a *ménàge à trois*."

menarchy (mɛ 'nɑːr ki) noun. formal and medical use. The time when a girl begins to menstruate. "The average age of *menarchy* among American girls is 12 years and four months."

menopause ('mɛ nə pɔz) noun. formal and general use. The end of a woman's childbearing years, when menstruation stops and the ovaries stop producing female sex hormones. "Most women enter *menopause* between forty-two and fifty-five years of age."

menstruation (mɛn 'stru ei ʃən) noun. formal. The monthly passing of discarded blood from the lining of the uterus. Also: **menses**

***mess** (mɛs) verb. euphemism. To have a bowel movement in a diaper, in one's underwear, or in some other inappropriate place. "The baby *messed* (in) his diaper." "The child *messed* her pants." The dog *messed* in the living room."

***mettle** ('mɛt əl) noun. slang 1. Manliness. 2. Semen.

micturate ('mɪk tʃyə reit) verb. formal and medical use. Urinate.

middle leg ('mɪd əl 'lɛg) noun. slang. The penis.

***milkers** ('mɪl kərz) noun, plural. slang. A woman's breasts.

***the Milky Way** (ðə 'mɪl ki 'wei) noun. slang. A woman's breasts.

M

missionary position ('mɪ ʃə nɛr i pə 'zɪ ʃən) noun. slang. The position for sexual intercourse in which the man lies on top of the woman. Missionaries from Christian churches came to Africa to run schools and teach religion. The natives, who preferred rear-entry intercourse were surprised at the face-to-face manner of the missionaries. They called it the *missionary position*.

miss a period (mɪs ə 'piː riː əd) verb phrase. general use. To *not* have a menstrual period on schedule. "Doctor, I *missed my period*. I think I might be pregnant."

***mistress** ('mɪ strɛs) noun. general use. A woman who has a permanent relationship with a man, but is not married to him, is his mistress. "I'd rather be a man's *mistress* than his wife," said Emily.

molest (mə 'lɛst) verb. general use. To harm or threaten a person in a sexual manner. "Many women do not walk outside alone at night. They are afraid of being *molested*." "Officer! Arrest that man! He *molested* me!"

molester; child molester (mə 'lɛs tər, tʃaɪld mə 'lɛs tər) noun. general use. A person who harms or threatens to harm another person (child) sexually.

Montezuma's revenge ('mɑn tə zuː məz rə 'vɛndʒ) noun. slang. Diarrhea, especially when one is a tourist in Mexico or some other Central or South American country. Montezuma was the last Aztec Mexican emperor whose empire was destroyed by Spanish invaders.

***monthly** ('mʌnθ li) noun. euphemism. Menstrual period. "Bonnie doesn't like to play tennis when she has her *monthly*."

***mood, to be in the** (tə biː ɪn ðə muːd) verb phrase. euphemism. To be ready for sexual activity. "She knew he was *in the mood* when he showed up with flowers for her."

***moon** (muːn) noun. slang. The buttocks. **moon**, **hang a moon** (hæŋ ə 'muːn) verb phrase. vulgar. To pull down one's underpants and bend over, showing one's buttocks out of a window. Also: **chuck a moon**.

*__mother__ ('mʌ ðər) noun. vulgar euphemism, now becoming commonly used. Short for *mother-fucker*. "Shut up you little *mother*." "Who's the *mother* that took my wallet?"

mother-fucker ('mʌ ðər 'fʌ kər) noun. vulgar. A detestable, hateful person. This word is among the most vulgar of American expressions to those who hear it for the first time. However, the original meaning–a person who fucks his mother–is lost when people hear the word many times. "Old Man Rather is the rottenest, meanest *mother-fucker* who ever walked on earth," said Charles. "You rotten *mother-fucker*! Get the hell out of here!" 2. An old friend; a buddy. "Marty, you old *mother-fucker*! It's good to see you!" "I was in big trouble until Al came along. That *mother-fucker* saved my life."

M.F. (ɛm ɛf) noun. Euphemism for *mother-fucker*, but still quite vulgar.

move one's bowels (muːv wunz baʊls) verb phrase. general use. Defecate. "I haven't *moved my bowels* for three days. I wonder if I should take a laxative."

*__muff__ (mʌf) noun. vulgar. A woman's pubic area.

*__muff-diving__ ('mʌf daɪ viŋ) noun phrase. vulgar. Cunnilingus. Oral sex; man's tongue on a woman's genitals.

N

*__napkin__ ('næp kɪn) noun. formal. Sanitary napkin, worn by a woman during her monthly period. British use: *baby diaper*.

*__neck__ (nɛk) verb. slang. To kiss and caress. "They went to a movie, sat in the back row, and *necked* through the whole show."

necrophiliac (nɛk ro 'fɪ liː æk) noun. formal. A person who has sexual fantasies or desires to have sex with a dead body.

N

neuter (ˈnuː ɒər) 1. adj. general use. Not male and not female. Not having sexual characteristics. 2. verb. euphemism. To castrate or spay an animal. To remove the sex glands so the animal cannot reproduce. "We had our cat *neutered*."

nipples (ˈnɪ pəls) noun, plural. general use. 1. The little bumps in the center of the breasts. 2. The rubber mouthpiece on a baby's bottle.

nocturnal emission (nɑk ˈtər nəl ɪ ˈmɪ ʃən) noun. formal. Ejaculation of semen during sleep while having a sex dream. Boys start having nocturnal emissions at around fourteen years of age.

nookie (ˈnʊ ki) noun. vulgar. 1. Sexual intercourse. 2. The vagina. "Sean went out looking for *nookie*." "How about a little *nookie* tonight?" he asked her.

***number one** (num bər ˈwʌn) noun. children's euphemism. Urine. "Daddy, I have to make *number one*."

***number two** (num bər tuː) noun. children's euphemism. Feces. **make number two; do number two** = defecate. "The baby did *number two* in his pants."

***nuts** (nʌts) noun, plural. 1. vulgar. Testicles. 2. slang. Expression of disgust or disappointment. "Oh *nuts*–the movie I wanted to see isn't playing anymore."

nymphomaniac (nɪm fou mei niː æk) noun. 1. formal and general use. A woman with an unusually strong desire for sexual intercourse. She may have many sex partners, and still not be satisfied. She is suffering from nymphomania. 2. slang. A strongly sexed woman.

O

obscene (ɑb ˈsiːn) adj. general use. Disgusting, offensive. Not acceptable to the moral standards of the community. Pictures of naked bodies may be considered obscene by one group of people, but beautiful by another group of people.

obscene language = vulgar language. Some people may think this book is *obscene*, and others will think it is educational.

obscenity (əb 'sɜ nə ti) noun. formal and general use. An obscene or disgusting thing. A vulgar word. "Ned shouted *obscenities* at the driver who had cut him off in traffic."

obstetrician (ɑb stə 'trɪ ʃən) noun. formal and general use. A doctor who delivers babies, and cares for pregnant women.

off-color (ɔːf 'kʌ lər) adj. slang. Having sexual meanings that are possibly offensive to some people. "George told an *off-color* joke at the meeting. No one laughed–it was the wrong place. There was a cold silence."

old maid (ould meid) noun. slang. derogatory. An older unmarried woman. This term has become *obsolete*. Many women, by their own choice, do not marry and there is no social penalty for this.

O

***one-eyed worm** (wʌn aɪd 'wərm) noun. slang. The penis. Also, **one-eyed pants mouse**; **one-eyed trouser trout**; **one-eyed zipper snake**.

one-night stand (wʌn naɪt stænd) noun. slang. A sexual relationship that lasts for only one evening. (This expression comes from show-business slang: A traveling show may spend only one night in a small town; this is called a one-night stand.) "Henry was tired of *one-night stands*; he wanted to meet a woman he could love and have a permanent relationship with."

opposite sex, the ('ɑ pə zət 'sɛks) noun. general use. The other sex. For a man, a woman is the opposite sex. "Teenagers begin to take great interest in the *opposite sex*."

oral-genital ('ɔː rəl 'dʒɛ nə təl) adj. formal. Mouth-to-penis or mouth-to-clitoris sexual stimulation. "Many couples enjoy *oral-genital* sex."

oral sex See above.

* words with additional meanings not listed

***organ** ('ɔːr gən) noun. euphemism. Sex organ. The penis.

orgasm ('ɔːr gæ zəm) noun. formal and general use. Sexual climax in male or female. The moment of ejaculation for a male; the rhythmic involuntary vaginal contractions in a female. "Jeannette had never experienced an *orgasm* until she met Joshua."

***orgy** ('ɔːr dʒi) noun. general use. 1. Excess (more than enough) activity in eating, sex, or other pleasures. 2. A party at which a great deal of uninhibited sexual activity occurs. Often used in a joking, exaggerated way.

outhouse ('aʊt haʊs) noun. slang. In the days before indoor plumbing, a small building (shack) in which there was a seat with a hole. The deep pit dug under it was the toilet.

out of wedlock ('aʊt əv 'wɛd lɑk) phrase. formal and general use. Referring to children born to an unmarried mother. "She had a child *out of wedlock*, but later married the father."

ova ('ou və) noun, plural. 1. formal and medical use. The full supply of a woman's reproductive cells. (singular form: **ovum**) 2. general use: egg. "A single *ovum* is released by the ovary each month."

ovary ('ou və ri) noun. formal and general use. The female organ that produces the ova. A woman has two ovaries, located in the *abdomen*. (See picture on page 85.)

***oven** ('ʌ vən) noun. slang. Womb, uterus. "He's got one kid already, and one in the *oven*." (That is, his wife is pregnant.)

***overcoat** ('ou vər kout) noun. slang. Condom.

ovulation (ɑ vyu 'lei ʃən) noun. formal and medical use. The monthly release of an ovum from the ovary. **ovulate** verb. "She took her temperature every day to find out when she was *ovulating*."

P

*__package__ ('pæ kɪdʒ) noun. vulgar slang. A man's genitals. "His bathing suit was tight, so she could see that he had a nice *package*."

*__pair__ (pɛər) noun. slang. A woman's breasts. "The barmaid has quite a *pair*, hasn't she?"

panther piss (pæn θər pɪs) noun. vulgar. Cheap, poor-quality whisky or beer.

panties ('pæn tiːz) noun, plural. general use. Women's or girls' underpants.

Pap smear ('pæp smiər) noun. formal and medical use. A test for cancer of the cervix. The doctor takes a small sample of the cells of the cervix of the uterus, to be tested in the laboratory. "Women are advised to have a *Pap smear* once a year."

*__party hat__ (pɑːr ti hæt) noun. slang. Condom.

pass gas (pæs 'gæs) verb phrase. general use. Expel gas from the rectum. Also, **pass air; pass wind**.

P

*__passion__ ('pæ ʃən) noun. general use. Great emotion. A strong desire for sex.

passionate ('pæ ʃə nət) adj. general use. Very emotional. Having intense feelings. (These may be anger, love, or sexual excitement.) "She is a *passionate* woman and she wants a *passionate* husband."

*__patch__ (pætʃ) noun. vulgar. Female.

pecker ('pɛ kər) noun. vulgar. The penis.

pecker tracks ('pɛ kər træks) noun. vulgar. Stains on the front of a man's clothes from dried semen.

peddle one's ass ('pɛ dəl wʌnz 'æs) verb phrase. vulgar. To sell sexual favors for money. Work as a prostitute.

pederast ('pɛ dər æst) noun. formal. A homosexual man who has relations with a young boy. **pederasty** ('pɛ dər æs ti) noun. formal. Sexual relations between a man and a young boy. "The police arrested the man and charged him with *pederasty*."

pedophilia (pɛ də 'fɪ liː ə) noun. formal. Loving children in a sexual way. A *pedophile* is a person who has sexual desires for children, and may molest them.

pee (piː) 1. verb. vulgar. Urinate. "The dog *pee'd* all over the floor." 2. noun. vulgar. Urine.

pee pee ('piː piː) 1. verb. children's word. Urinate. "Mommy, I have to *pee pee* real bad." 2. noun. children's word. Urine. "There's *pee pee* on the floor." 3. noun. children's word. Penis.

peeping Tom (piː pɪŋ 'tɑm) noun. slang. A person who gets pleasure from secretly looking (peeping) into windows to watch others get undressed, or watch couples engage in sexual activates. A *voyeur*.

pelvic examination (pɛl vɪk ɛg 'zæ mə nei ʃən) noun. formal and general use. An internal examination of a woman's reproductive organs. "Debra went to the doctor for an annual *pelvic examination* and Pap smear."

pendejo (pɛn 'de ho) noun. vulgar. 1. Spanish = pubic hair. 2. A very stupid, clumsy person.

***penetration** (pɛ nə 'trei ʃən) noun. formal. The act of entering; the entering of the vagina by the penis. "*Penetration* is difficult or impossible without a firm erection of the penis."

***period** ('pɪr iː əd) noun. general use. The menstrual period. The time of the month when a woman's uterus releases the supply of blood that has been building up in it. "Helen's *period* usually lasted six last days." "Her *period* was late."

miss a period (mɪs ə 'pɪr iː əd) verb phrase. general use. Not have a monthly period. "Sarah *missed her period* so she bought a pregnancy test kit at the drug store."

perversion (pər 'vər ʒən) noun. general use. A sexual practice that is considered unusual and unacceptable to a majority of people. "Homosexuality was considered a *perversion* in American culture until recently. Most experts now say that it is a way of being that people are born with, and is not an illness to correct."

***pervert** ('pər vərt) noun. general use. A person who engages in some form of perversion or unnatural sexual activity. Derogatory.

***pet** (pɛt) verb. slang. To caress and fondle (touch) skin, breasts, and genitals.

***peter** ('piːt ər) noun. children's word. The penis.

piddle (pɪd əl) verb. euphemism. Urinate. "The puppy piddled whenever it was excited."

piece (piːs) noun. vulgar. Short for piece of ass or piece of tail. "How about a little *piece* tonight?"

piece of ass (piːs əv 'æs) noun. vulgar. 1. A woman as a sexual object. "That new receptionist looks like a nice *piece of ass*," said Patrick. 2. An act of sexual intercourse. "I'm going down to town and get me a *piece of ass*," said the cowboy."

piece of tail (piːs əv 'teil) noun. vulgar. Same as *piece of ass*.

piece of shit (piːs əv 'ʃɪt)/(piːs ə 'ʃɪt) noun. vulgar. Any worthless, useless thing. "That new motorcycle I bought is a *piece of shit*; it has been in the repair shop six times since I got it." "Julie felt like a *piece of shit* when she arrived at the party. She was the only person who had not brought a gift."

piles (paɪəlz) noun. general use. Hemorrhoids. Swollen or varicose veins in the region of the anus.

pill, the (pɪl) noun. general use. A birth control pill, usually taken daily. "Silvia was on *the pill*, so she wasn't afraid of getting pregnant."

P

pimp (pɪmp) noun. slang. A man who manages one or more prostitutes. He finds customers for her, and bails her out of jail when she is arrested. She in turn pays him nearly all, or a large percentage of the money she makes.

pimpmobile (pɪmp mou 'biːl) noun. slang. A very expensive car, often a Cadillac, of a wild color–such as gold, lavender, or pink.

pinch a loaf (pɪntʒ ə 'louf) verb phrase. vulgar. Defecate.

***pipe** (paɪp) noun. slang. Penis.

pish (pɪʃ) verb. children's word. Urinate.

piss (pɪs) 1. verb. vulgar. Urinate. 2. noun. vulgar. Urine.

piss away (pɪs ə 'wei) verb phrase. vulgar. To waste. To spend money without thinking. "Philip inherited a fortune from his rich uncle but he *pissed it away* on cars and fancy women."

pissed off (pɪst 'ɔːf) adj. vulgar. Angry. "Ted gets *pissed off* when another car cuts him off in traffic." "That *pisses me off*." "That really makes me angry."

p.o.'d (piː 'oud) slang. Euphemism, abbreviation for pissed off. "There's no need for you to get *p.o.'d*," he said, " I'll pay for the things I broke."

pisser ('pɪs ər) noun. slang. 1. A remarkable, daring, or amusing person or child. "Young Willy is a real *pisser*. He's only four years old but he knows how to flirt with girls." 2. A difficult job. "Fixing the refrigerator was a real *pisser*. We didn't have any of the right tools."

piss on that! (pɪs ɑn 'ðæt) exclamation. vulgar. An expression of disagreement or disapproval.

piss poor (pɪs puːr) adj. vulgar. Poor; of very low quality. "That was a *piss poor* dinner, considering what we paid for it."

piss and vinegar (pɪs ən ˈvɪ nə gər) noun phrase. vulgur. Energy, independent thinking; ability to shock others. "My grandfather was ninety years old, but he was still full of *piss and vinegar*. He often did and said things that shocked us kids."

platonic (plə ˈtɑ nək) adjective. general use. This refers to a friendship between male and female that does not include sex. "Laura had a *platonic* relationship with Victor for years."

play "hide the sausage" (plei ˈhaɪd ðə ˈsɔː sidʒ) verb phrase. slang. Have sexual intercourse. Male to male friend: "I'm going home to *play "hide the sausage"* with my wife.

play with oneself (ˈplei wɪθ wʌn sɛlf) verb phrase. slang. Masturbate. Contrast with play by oneself. To play alone, without friends. Be careful. "The child played *by* himself (or herself)" has no dangerous meanings. But "The child played *with* himself (or herself)" means he or she was *masturbating*.

P

***play pocket pool** (plei ˈpɑ kət puːl) verb phrase. slang. To masturbate or stimulate oneself through the pants pocket.

play the skin flute (plei ðə ˈskɪn fluːt) verb phrase. slang. Oral sex. Fellatio. Suck a penis. Also, **play the (pink) piccolo**.

***poop, poo poo** (puːp, ˈpuː puː) children's word. 1. noun: Feces. 2. verb: To defecate.

poop chute (puːp ʃuːt) noun. vulgar, humorous use. The anus.

pornography (pɔːr ˈnɑ grə fi) noun. formal and general use. Stories, movies, books, and pictures that tell about or show scenes of sexual activities. The purpose of pornography is to get a person sexually excited.

pornographic (pɔːr nɑ 'græ fɪk) adj. form. "Nellie enjoyed *pornographic* movies." "The man at the candy store was arrested for selling *pornography* to children."

***possess** (pə 'zɛs) verb. euphemism. Have sexual intercourse. This word is found in women's romance novels, and in books printed before it was legal to use stronger language. "He carried her to his bed, and there he *possessed* her."

posterior (pɑs 'tiər iː ər) noun. euphemism. The buttocks.

***potency** ('pou tən si) noun. formal and general use. A man's ability to perform sexual intercourse. "Wally's *potency* increased when he improved his diet and started taking vitamins."

pot to piss in noun. vulgar. The basic things that money can buy. This term is most often used in the negative: "We were so poor, we didn't have a *pot to piss in*."

potty (pɑt i) noun. children's word. Toilet. A small toilet especially for training little children. It has a removable pot.

powder room ('paʊ dər ruːm) noun. euphemism. The bathroom. This word is used by women, generally in restaurants and other public places. They may excuse themselves to go "powder my nose" (apply face make up). A euphemism for using the toilet.

pregnancy ('prɛg nən si) noun. formal and general use. The nine month period during which a baby grows in its mother's uterus; *gestation*. "She had a very easy *pregnancy* and an easy delivery."

pregnant ('prɛg nənt) adjective. formal and general use. Having a baby develop in one's uterus. "Naomi was delighted to be *pregnant*." Sometimes both the father-to-be and the mother-to-be are referred to as "the *pregnant* couple."

premature ejaculation (priː mə 'tʃʊər ˌ dʒæ kyu 'lei ʃən) noun. formal. This is when a man reaches a climax (ejaculation) before or shortly after the penis enters the vagina.

***prick** (prɪk) noun. vulgar. 1. The penis. 2. A disliked (male) person.

prime one's pump (praɪm wʌnz 'pʌmp) verb. slang. To get one sexually excited.

privates, private parts (praɪ vəts, praɪ vət pɑːrts) noun, plural. euphemism. The genital area of a man or woman. "Wanda told her children to tell her, or the teacher or principal if anyone tried to touch them in their *private parts.*"

proctologist (prɑk 'tɑ lə dʒɪst) noun. formal. A doctor who specializes in treating diseases of the rectum and anus.

procurer (prou 'kyur ər) noun. formal. A person who persuades others to work as prostitutes. One who finds a prostitute for a customer.

profanity (proː 'fæ nə ti) noun. general use. 1. Religious taboo words forbidden by church teachings. 2. Vulgar words and expressions. "Don't use *profanity* in the classroom."

promiscuous (prou 'mɪ skyuː əs)/(prə 'mɪ skyuː əs) adj. general use. This word describes a person who has sexual relations with many different partners, and who is not very careful in choosing a partner.

prophylactic (prou fə 'læk tɪk)/(prɑ fə 'læk tɪk) noun. general use. A condom. A birth control device, also used to reduce the spread of disease.

***proposition** (prɑ pə 'zɪ ʃən) 1. verb. euphemism. To ask another person to have sex. 2. noun. euphemism. The suggestion of sexual activity. "Jane was very attractive. Men would walk up to her on the street and *proposition* her." "Beverly was shocked when her supervisor *propositioned* her. She reported this as sexual harassment."

P

* words with additional meanings not listed

prostate ('prɑ steit) noun. formal and general use. In a man, the gland that surrounds the urethra near the bladder.

puberty ('pyuː bər ti) noun. formal and general use. The time when children develop into adults. "In the U.S. the average girl reaches *puberty* at age eleven; the average boy achieves it at fourteen."

pubic area ('pyuː bɪk 'ɛər iː ə) noun. formal and general use. The crotch. The lower part of the abdomen.

pubic hair ('pyuː bɪk hɛər) noun. formal and general use. The hair in the pubic area.

pudendum (puː 'dɛn dəm) noun. formal and medical use. The vulva. The external female genital area.

***pussy** ('pʊ si) noun. vulgar. The vagina and vulva. **Have some pussy.** (male use) To have sexual intercourse.

pussy-whipped ('pʊ si wɪpt) adjective. vulgar. Unhappily married. Bossed around by a woman. Obedient because of fear of losing one's mate.

***put out** (for) (pʊt 'aʊt) verb. slang. Give sexual favors (usually said of a woman). To allow someone to have sexual intercourse. "Whenever Gerty was pissed off at her husband, she wouldn't *put out* for him."

Q

***queen** (kwiːn) noun. slang. A male homosexual with feminine appearance and manners.

***queer** (kwiər) noun. slang. derogatory. A homosexual. adj. **Homosexual.**

***quickie** ('kwɪ ki) noun. slang. A short session of sexual intercourse. "How about a *quickie* before going to the movies?" he asked. "No, thanks" she said.

quim (kwɪm) noun. vulgar. Vagina.

R

rabbit, have some (hæv sʌm 'ræ bɪt) verb phrase. slang. Be sexually active, like a rabbit.

*__rag__ (ræg) noun. slang. Sanitary napkin. **to be on the rag =** (for a woman) To have her period. To be irritable and bitchy. (This may be said even of men.)

rape (reip) verb. general use. To force sexual intercourse with someone. Rape is a crime.

rape artist ('reip 'ɑːrt ɪst) noun. slang. A man who rapes women. A *rapist*.

rapist ('reip ɪst) noun. formal and general use. A man who forces sexual intercourse with a woman. "The police are looking for the *rapist* who attacked and molested two women in the park recently."

*__rear; rear end__ (riər; riər 'ɛnd) noun. euphemism. The buttocks.

rectum ('rɛk təm) noun. formal and general use. The last part of the large colon, or large intestine. "The waste material is stored in the *rectum* until it is expelled from the body."

red-light district (rɛd 'laɪt dɪs trɪkt) noun. euphemism. An area in a city where there are houses of prostitution. "While he was in Amsterdam, he went to visit the *red-light district*."

*__relations, (to) have...with__ (tə hæv rə 'lei ʃənz wɪθ) verb phrase. euphemism. Have sexual intercourse. "The church teaches young people that it is a mistake to have sexual *relations* before they are married."

relieve oneself (rə 'liːv wʌn sɛlf) verb phrase. euphemism. Urinate. "Can we stop at the next gas station? If I don't *relieve myself*, my bladder will explode."

rest room ('rɛst ruːm) noun. euphemism. A toilet in a public place such as a restaurant, gas station, theater, etc.

R

* words with additional meanings not listed

rhythm method ('rɪðm mɛθ əd) noun. general use.
A method of birth control. The partners have sexual intercourse only during the *safe*, or non-fertile, days of the woman's menstrual cycle.

ride the cotton pony (raɪd ðə kɑt ən 'pou ni) verb phrase. vulgar. 1. To wear a sanitary napkin while menstruating. 2. To have sex with a woman who is menstruating.

***rim** (rɪm) verb. vulgar. To lick the area around the anus during sex play.

***rocks** (rɑks) noun, plural. vulgar. The testicles.

get one's rocks off (gɛt wʌnz 'rɑks ɔːf) verb phrase. vulgar. 1. Ejaculate; reach a sexual climax. 2. Enjoy oneself very much by participating in some hobby or activity. "Pat *gets his rocks off* going to the horse races and betting on the ponies."

Rocky Mountain oysters (rɑk ki maʊn tən 'ɔɪ stərz) noun, plural. Testicles.

***root** (ruːt) noun. slang. A man's penis.

***rubber** ('rʌb ər) noun. slang. A condom.

***rump** (rʌmp) noun. slang. The buttocks.

rump ranger ('rʌmp rein dʒer) noun. slang. A homosexual male.

***run around** (rʌn ə 'raʊnd) verb. euphemism. Have sexual relations with several partners although married to another person. "Tom has a beautiful wife. I can't understand why he *runs around*."

***runs** (rʌnz) noun. slang. Diarrhea. (One has to run to the bathroom quickly when one has diarrhea.) "Eva ate green apples and they gave her the *runs*." "Dean stayed home from work because he had the *runs*."

S

S.B.D. (ɛs biː diː) noun. vulgar. **Silent But Deadly**. A quiet and very bad-smelling fart.

sadist ('seid ɪst) noun. general use. A person who gets sexual pleasure from giving pain to his or her partner. **sadism** ('seid ɪ zəm) noun. general use. A *perversion*. Sexual pleasure is gotten from causing pain to another person.

sado-masochism ('seid ou 'mæ sə kɪ zəm) noun. formal and general use. A sexual perversion in which one partner enjoys causing pain (the sadist), and the other enjoys being hurt (the masochist). Also: **S & M**.

***safety** ('seif ti) noun. euphemism. A condom.

sanitary napkin ('sæ nə tei ri 'næp kɪn) noun. formal and general use. A pad of cotton and gauze used to absorb menstrual blood. It is worn by a woman, in the crotch of her panties.

***satisfy** ('sæt ɪs faɪː) verb. euphemism. To cause one's partner to reach a sexual climax.

***to be satisfied** (tə biː 'sæt ɪs faɪd) verb phrase. euphemism. Have a sexual climax, and become relaxed.

S

***scam** (skæm) verb. slang. To go looking for members of the opposite sex.

scammer ('skæ mər) noun. slang. A person (usually male) who has sex with a series of partners, with no regard for their feelings.

***schlong** (ʃlaŋ) noun. vulgar. The penis.

schmuck (ʃmʌk) noun. 1. slang. A stupid person. 2. vulgar. The penis. (Yiddish word) A: "What does she like about Marshall? He's such a *schmuck*!" B: "Maybe it's because he has a big *schmuck*!"

screaming fairy ('skriː mɪŋ 'fɛə ri) noun. slang, offensive. A homosexual who is very *obviously* a homosexual. He wears beautiful, brightly colored clothing, and walks and speaks in an exaggeratedly female manner.

***screw** (skruː) verb. 1. vulgar. Have sexual intercourse with. "Larry is oversexed," complained his wife. "All he thinks of is *screwing*." 2. slang. Cheat in a business deal. "Don't do business with that company; they'll *screw* you if they can."

screw around (skruː ə 'raʊnd) verb phrase. vulgar. 1. To have many sexual partners; to be unfaithful to one's own partner. "Karl is married, but he still *screws around*." 2. To waste time. "Stop *screwing around* and get the job started."

screw up (skruː 'ʌp) verb. slang. 1. Make many mistakes; do an unsatisfactory job; do something incompetently. 2. Cause something to fail. "The shipping department *screwed up* again. They sent the wrong product to the customer." "I wanted to go to the beach this weekend, but the bad weather *screwed up* my plans."

screw with (skruː wɪθ) verb phrase. vulgar. To cheat in a business or social matter. "Nobody *screws with* Old Mr. Zappo without getting paid back double."

screw you! (skruː 'yuː) exclamation. vulgar. An angry reply to someone = ***Fuck you***, but somewhat less vulgar.

scrotum ('skrout əm) noun. formal and general use. The sac that contains the testicles.

***scum** (skʌm) noun. vulgar. Semen.

scumbag (skʌm bæg) noun. vulgar. 1. A condom; a rubber prophylactic used for birth control. 2. A very disliked, low, dirty, dishonest person. "Why does Gloria hang around with those *scumbags*?"

***seat** (siːt) noun. euphemism. The buttocks.

see a man about a horse verb phrase. slang. Go to the bathroom.

***seed** (siːd) noun. euphemism. Sperm. Characteristics that can be inherited genetically.

self-abuse (sɛlf ə 'byuːs) noun. euphemism. Masterbation; touching one's own genitals to get sexual pleasure. This term was used many years ago when mothers thought that it was harmful for children to masturbate. They told their sons that "*self-abuse*" would make them blind. In one joke, a boy asks "Is it all right if I do it only until I need glasses?"

semen ('siː mən) noun. formal and general use. The white liquid produced in the male reproductive organs. The fluid that carries the sperm.

sex (sɛks) noun. general use. 1. Gender. Maleness or femaleness. "What *sex* are the new puppies?" "Can the doctor tell the *sex* of the baby before it is born?" 2. An act of sexual intercourse. "Mike always enjoyed *sex* before breakfast." "Larry would like to *have sex* at least three times a week, but his wife isn't interested in *sex* that often." 3. The general topic of sexual matters. "All she talks about is *sex*."

sex appeal ('sɛks ə 'piːl) noun. general use. Attractiveness. "James has a lot of *sex appeal*; the girls are always around him."

sex drive ('sɛks draɪv) noun. general use. The impulse or need that causes a person to desire sexual relations. "Some people have a greater *sex drive* than others." "Does a woman's *sex drive* increase as she gets older?"

sex fiend ('sɛks fiːnd) noun. general use. 1. Rapist, child molester, or sexual pervert. 2. (humorous) A person with a very strong sex drive.

sex maniac ('sɛks 'mei niː æk) noun. general use. 1. Rapist, child molester, or sex fiend. A dangerous person who may murder or seriously harm his victims. 2. (humorous) A person with a very strong sex drive.

S

sex organs ('sɛks 'ɔːr gənz) noun, plural. formal and general use. Organs of reproduction; gonads. "The worm has both male and female *sex organs*." (In mammals, the male *sex organs* are the penis and testicles. The female *sex organs* are the vagina, ovaries, and uterus.)

sex symbol ('sɛks 'sɪm bəl) noun. general use. A very attractive famous male or female. "Who is a famous *sex symbol* in the movies today?"

sexual harassment ('sɛk ʃyuː əl hə 'ræs mənt) noun phrase. general use. Actions or language between men and women that are not appropriate at school or at work, and not welcome. Using one's position of power as employer or supervisor to demand sexual favors. Telling sex jokes, making sexual comments, displaying sexual materials at the work or school area.

sexual intercourse ('sɛk ʃyuː əl 'ɪn tər kɔːrs) noun. formal and general use. The act of union between male and female. "In humans, the penis enters the vagina during *sexual intercourse*."

sexy ('sɛk si) adj. general use. 1. Attractive, in a sexual way. "He has a *sexy* voice." "That's a *sexy* bathing suit." "Wanda is a *sexy* woman." 2. Aroused, interested in having sex. "Isaac was feeling *sexy*."

shack up (ʃæk 'ʌp) verb. slang, may be offensive. To live together without being legally married. (A shack is a cheaply made house.) Kelly has been *shacking up* with David for over a year."

***shaft** (ʃæft) noun. slang. Penis.

shaft; give someone the shaft ('gɪv sʌm wʌn ðe 'ʃæft) verb phrase. 1. vulgar (before 1960) To have anal intercourse. 2. slang (current use) To betray, double cross, deceive or reject someone or treat someone cruelly. "The company gave poor Fred *the shaft* today–after 25 years of loyal service, they reduced his pay and gave his office to a new employee."

***shake hands with a friend** (ʃeik 'hændz wɪθ ə 'frɛnd) verb phrase. slang. 1. Urinate. 2. Masturbate.

she-man (ʃiː mæn) noun. slang. Homosexual, particularly an effeminate man. Also, she-male.

shit (ʃɪt) noun. vulgar. 1. Feces. 2. Junk, worthless things. 3. Heroin (narcotic drug) 4. verb. vulgar. Defecate. 5. To tell lies, exaggerate, fool. "You wouldn't *shit me*, would you?" 6. **Shit!** Exclamation of anger, disgust, or disappointment.

Shit is one of the most versatile words in English. It can be used as a noun, adjective, or verb, and appears in dozens of idioms and expressions. It is the most common word to express sudden anger or frustration.

act as though one's shit didn't smell bad verb phrase. vulgar. To think that one is much better than others and not see one's own human shortcomings and faults. Joan is always pointing out her friends' mistakes; she *acts as though her own shit doesn't smell bad*.

apeshit ('eip ʃɪt) adj. vulgar. 1. Angry in a crazy, wild, uncontrollable way. "When Ramon saw his best friend dancing with his girl, he went *apeshit*." 2. Very enthusiastic. Excited and interested in something. "Jerry goes *apeshit* when he's around racing cars."

S

beat the shit out of ('biːt ðə ʃɪt aʊt əv) verb phrase. vulgar. 1. To physically beat someone severely, theoretically to the point that they lose control of their bowels. "When my father found out I had lied to him, he *beat the shit out of* me." 2. To defeat by a large margin. "The Giants *beat the shit out of* the Red Socks. The score was 12 to 1."

crock of shit (krɑk əv ʃɪt) noun. vulgar. A lot of lies.

Don't give me that shit! expression. Vulgar. Don't tell me those lies; don't do those acts I don't like.

* words with additional meanings not listed

eat this shit verb phrase. vulgar. Accept insults and punishments without protesting. "Maybe the boss expects me to *eat this shit*, but I'll quit my job first."

full of shit (fʊl əv ʃɪt)/(fʊl ə ʃɪt) adj. phrase. vulgar. Always telling lies or exaggerated stories that are not based on the true facts. Wrong ideas; empty talk. "Don't listen to Ben. He's *full of shit*."

get one's shit together verb phrase. vulgar. To get organized; to have a goal in life and be in action. "I'll get a job as soon as I *get my shit together*."

give a shit verb phrase. vulgar. 1. To care for, be concerned about, have an interest in, etc. 2. Don't/doesn't give a shit. To have no interest in or regard for something. "Harry is usually late to work because he just *doesn't give a shit* whether he keeps the job or not."

holy shit! ('hoʊ li ʃɪt) interjection. vulgar. Expression of surprise or discovery. "*Holy shit*! This is a treasure map!"

horse shit ('hɔːrs ʃɪt) noun. vulgar. 1. Horse droppings. 2. Lies, false stories. "Don't give me that *horse shit* about being out of money. Pay me now."

hot shit (hɑt ʃɪt) noun. vulgar. Very important. (Said sarcastically.) "Betty thinks she's *hot shit*, but she really has no power in this office."

I'm so happy I could shit. expression. vulgar. 1. I'm very happy. 2. I'm really miserable. The meaning depends on the context and the tone of voice.

little shit ('lɪ ɒəl ʃɪt) noun. vulgar. 1. A very unimportant person, disliked and small in size. "Who does that *little shit* think he is, Napoleon?" 2. An active and remarkable little boy. Said proudly: "Look at that *little shit* swim! He's faster than Tarzan."

lower than whale shit adjective phrase. vulgar. Depressed, sad, humiliated, regretful. Roy lost his job, his girlfriend left him, and his car broke down. "How do you feel?" asked his friend. "*Lower than whale shit*." he said. "And that's at the bottom of the ocean."

no shit! interjection. vulgar. Exclamation of surprise or disbelief at what someone has just said. Andrew: "My cousin just married Va Va Voom the famous movie star." Ben: "*No shit*! How did he meet her?" Said sarcastically, "No shit" means "You're not telling me anything new. I can see it for myself; everybody already knows that." Joseph: "It's really hot today." Renee: "*No shit*, Einstein."

not know shit from Shinola
('nɑt nou ʃɪt frʌm ʃaɪ 'nou lə) verb phrase. vulgar. To be very stupid. "That new employee *doesn't know shit from Shinola*; he can't hammer a nail in straight."

piece of shit (pi:s əv 'ʃɪt) noun phrase. vulgar. A worthless, poorly made thing. "Why did you pay twenty thousand dollars for that car? It's not worth it; *it's a piece of shit*."

pile of shit (paɪl əv 'ʃɪt) noun phrase. vulgar. A lot of lies.

sack of shit (sæk əv 'ʃɪt) noun phrase. vulgar. Lies; worthless stuff.

scare the shit out of someone idiom. vulgar. To frighten someone very badly.

scared shitless (skeird 'ʃɪt ləs) adj. vulgar. Very frightened.

shit for the birds ('ʃɪt fər ðə 'bərdz) noun phrase. vulgar. Worthless idea or thing. "I don't think much of that suggestion you made. It's *shit for the birds*."

S

shit a brick (ʃɪt ə 'brɪk) verb phrase. vulgar. 1. Expel a large turd. 2. Do something very difficult. "We had to *shit bricks* to build this bridge." 3. Be very surprised, upset, or angry. "When Clark learned that we had gotten the prize, he was ready to *shit a brick*."

Shit Creek; Shit's Creek (ʃɪt kriːk, ʃɪts kriːk) noun. vulgar. A river made of shit. A very difficult position to be in. "They were up *Shit Creek* without a paddle." (They were unable to get out of severe difficulties.)

shit-eating grin (ʃɪt iːt ɪŋ 'grɪn) noun phrase. vulgar. A big smile, usually of pride. "Nick walked in the door with this big *shit-eating grin* on his face. We knew he had won the contest."

shit face ('ʃɪt feis) noun. vulgar. Ugly person. Used as an insult.

shit-faced ('ʃɪt feist) adj. vulgar. Drunk.

shit fit noun. vulgar. A great emotional upset. "When he heard that his son had borrowed his car without asking, he had a *shit fit*."

Shit or get off the pot (pot = toilet) vulgar. If you are not using the toilet, get off so that someone else may use it. This expression means, *don't waste our time*; *take action*.

Shit happens expression. vulgar. You can expect bad things to happen. That's life. Don't get too surprised or upset. (Sign on bumper stickers, T-shirts, etc.)

shit head ('ʃɪt hɛd) noun. vulgar. A stupid person.

shit hole ('ʃɪt houl) noun. vulgar. A poor, dirty, undesirable house, home, place. "We lived in this *shit hole* for three years before we earned enough to move to a better apartment."

S

shit list ('ʃɪt lɪst) noun. vulgar. A list (imaginary) of people at whom one is angry and whom one will avoid in the future, or punish, or cause trouble for. "Don't expect favors from Mr. Wilson. Ever since you insulted his wife, he has had you on his *shit list*."

shitload ('ʃɪt loud) noun. vulgar. A large amount. "I have a *shitload* of work to do tonight."

shit out of luck ('ʃɪt aut əv 'lʌk) adjective phrase. vulgar. Good luck has come to an end. Bad luck. "We tried to find an all-night drugstore, but we were *shit out of luck*." This may be said more politely as "We were **S.O.L.**"

shit (in) one's pants verb phrase. vulgar. To feel great fear. "Don just about *shit his pants* when he saw the bear."

shit on a shingle ('ʃɪt ɑn ə 'ʃɪŋ gəl) noun. vulgar. 1. Barbecued beef on a bun (round bread). (A shingle is a thin, flat piece of wood or tar paper used on the roof of a house.) 2. Army use: creamed chipped beef on toast.

(the) shits noun. vulgar. Diarrhea; loose stools; the runs. "Marshall always gets *the shits* when he eats raisins."

shitty ('ʃɪ ti) adj. vulgar. Lousy, no-good, worthless. "How was the movie?" "*Shitty*."

shovel the shit ('ʃʌ vəl ðə 'ʃɪt) verb phrase. vulgar. Tell lies. "Dan is good at *shoveling the shit*. He'd be a great salesman or politician."

tough shit! ('tʌf 'ʃɪt) interjection. vulgar. Exclamation showing that one does not feel sorry for someone who has a problem. Too bad. "But I must get my car back today." "*Tough shit!* There are ten people ahead of you."

T.S. (tiː ɛs) vulgar euphemism. *Tough shit!*

S

when the shit hits the fan (wɛn ðə ˈʃɪt hɪts ðə ˈfæn) idiom. vulgar. A time of great upset affecting many people involved in an activity. It is based on an old joke: There was a drunk in a barroom, and he had to go to the bathroom. He went upstairs, but could not find the men's room. He saw a hole in the floor, and he decided to do his business (defecate) into the hole. Then he went downstairs and saw the room covered with brown. No one was at the bar, and there was a terrible smell. He called out, "Where is everybody?" The bartender, who had been hiding under the bar asked him, "Where were you when the shit hit the fan?" Current use: "Ned knew his boss was going to be questioned by the police. He did not want to be around when the shit hit the fan, so he quit his job."

***shoot off** verb. vulgar. Ejaculate.

shoot one's wad (ʃuːt wʌnz ˈwɑd) verb phrase. vulgar. Ejaculate.

***short arm** (ʃɔːrt ɑːrm) noun. slang. The penis.

short-arm inspection verb phrase. slang. Army usage. A medical examination to check for venereal disease.

short ice (ʃɔːrt aɪs) noun. slang. Pornographic; "dirty" pictures, readers, etc.

Shove it up your ass! (ʃʌv ɪt ʌp yər æs) expression. vulgar. An exclamation of anger. "I don't want your opinion. You can *shove it up your ass* for all I care."

sitz bath (sɪtz bæθ) noun. general use. A warm water bath in which one sits. There may be medication in the water to treat sores, hemorrhoids, or other problems that affect the genital or anal region.

sixty-nine (sɪks ti ˈnaɪn) noun. vulgar euphemism. Oral-genital relations. Fellatio and cunnilingus (at the same time). The man's and woman's bodies appear to be like the numbers 6 and 9.

skinny-dip ('skɪ ni dɪp) verb. slang. Go swimming without a bathing suit. "They went skinny-dipping in the pool after midnight."

Slam, bam, thank you, Ma'am (slæm bæm θæŋ kyuː mæm) expression. slang. Very quick sexual intercourse, without pleasure for the female partner. Also: **Wham, bam, thank you Ma'am**.

sleep around (sliːp ə 'raʊnd) verb. euphemism. Have casual sexual relations with several partners.

sleep with (sliːp wɪθ) verb. euphemism. Have sexual intercourse with. "Sabrina bragged that she had *slept with* many famous men."

slut (slʌt) noun. slang, derogatory. (often used in anger) A woman who has sexual relations with many men and does not use any judgment in choosing her partners. "You filthy *slut*! Get out of my life!"

smallest room noun. slang. The bathroom.

***snatch** (snætʃ) noun. vulgar. The vagina.

***socialize** ('soʊ ʃə laɪz) verb. euphemism. Have sex.

sodomy ('sɑ də mi) noun. formal and general use. Any sex act other than intercourse between male and female, especially anal intercourse.

S

sodomize ('sɑ də maɪz) verb. formal. To have sodomy with. **Sodomist**. noun. formal. A person who performs *sodomy*.

***soil** (sɔɪl) verb. euphemism. To make dirty; to have a bowel movement. "The baby has *soiled* her diaper." "He got so scared when he saw the ghost that he *soiled* his pants."

son of a bitch (sʌn əv ə 'bɪtʃ) noun. vulgar. A disliked person. A person who treats other people badly. (*bitch* = female dog.)

S.O.B. (ɛs oʊ biː) noun. slang = *son of a bitch*. (Not vulgar in the abbreviated form.)

* words with additional meanings not listed

spay (spei) verb. formal, medical, and general use. To do an operation on a female cat or dog so she cannot have babies; alter. Past tense: **spayed** (speid). "The vet is going to *spay* our dog."

sperm (spərm) noun. general use. The male sex cells. "About 500,000 *sperm* are contained in one teaspoon of semen."
spermatozoa (spər ˈmæ tə zoː ə) noun. formal. Sperm.

spermicide (ˈspər mə saɪd) noun. formal and general use. Something that kills sperm: a birth control foam, jelly, or suppository.

***squelch** (skweltʃ) noun. slang: homosexual use. A sex act without affection.

***stacked** (stækt) adj. slang. Have large breasts. "Lorraine is really *stacked*. She wears a size 40-E bra."
stay in the closet verb phrase. slang. Not tell one's family and associates that one is gay. Hide one's sexual behavior from others in one's life.

***sterile** (ˈstɛr əl) adj. formal and general use. Unable to have children. Not fertile.

sterility (stə ˈrɪ lə ti) noun. formal and general use. Inability to have children.

***stern** (stərn) noun. slang euphemism. The buttocks. (The rear part of a boat.)

stinker (ˈstɪŋk ər) noun. vulgar. A fart; an expulsion of intestinal gas. "She let out a real *stinker* at the bar."

***stool** (stuːl) noun. formal and medical use. Feces. "The doctor gave his patient a kit for collecting a *stool* sample to bring to the laboratory for testing."

***stork** (stɔːrk) noun. euphemism. The deliverer of babies. (Long ago, people were embarrassed to tell children how babies were made. They told them that the stork (a bird with a very long beak) brings babies. The stork is still a symbol of the birth of a baby. "Mr. and Mrs. Walters are expecting *a visit from the stork*."

***straight** (streit) adj. slang. 1. Heterosexual. Attracted to the opposite sex; not homosexual. "Walter seems effeminate (like a woman), but he's completely *straight*." 2. Having no unusual sexual needs or desires. Not perverted.

street-walker ('stri:t wɔ:k ər) noun. slang. A prostitute.

suck (sʌk) verb. vulgar. Perform fellatio. *Suck my dick!* Exclamation of anger similar in intensity to "*Shove it up your ass!*"

sugar plum fairy ('ʃʊ gər plʌm 'fɛər i) noun. slang, derogatory. An effeminate gay person.

swallow a watermelon seed ('swɑ lou ə 'wʌt ər mɛl ən 'si:d) verb phrase. slang. Become pregnant. "What happened to your wife? Did she *swallow a watermelon seed*?"

swap spit (swɑp 'spɪt) verb phrase. slang. Kiss.

***swing** (swɪŋ) verb. slang. Exchange sexual partners. "Before the days of AIDS, there were stories of married couples who got together to '*swing*' for the evening."

swing both ways (swɪŋ bouθ 'weiz) verb phrase. slang. To be bisexual. To enjoy sexual relations with one's own sex as well as with the opposite sex. "Bruce *swings both ways*."

***swinger** ('swɪŋ ər) noun. slang. 1. A person who goes to many parties and other social events. 2. A person who has more than one sex partner, is bi-sexual, or is willing to experiment sexually.

***swingers** noun, plural. slang. 1. Testicles. 2. A woman's breasts that "swing" when she jogs or runs.

***swish** (swɪʃ) verb. slang. To walk with a very effeminate manner (like a woman). Said of homosexual men. "Mark *swished* in wearing a pink suit and flowered shirt."

syphilis ('sɪ fə ləs) noun. formal, medical and general use. A serious disease that is spread through sexual contact. A venereal disease.

* words with additional meanings not listed

T

T & A (tiː ən ei) noun, plural. vulgar. *Tits and asses*. Breasts and buttocks. "Let's go downtown and watch the *T & A* go by.

***tail** (teil) noun. 1. euphemism. The buttocks. 2. vulgar. The vagina.

piece of tail (piːs əv teil) noun. vulgar. An act of sexual intercourse.

take a crap (teik ə 'kræp) verb phrase. vulgar. Defecate.

take a dump (teik ə 'dʌmp) verb phrase. vulgar. Defecate.

take a leak (teik ə 'liːk) verb phrase. vulgar. Urinate.

take a shit (teik ə 'ʃɪt) verb phrase. vulgar. Defecate.

tampon ('tæm pɑn) noun. general use. A tube of cotton that is inserted in the vagina to absorb menstrual blood. "She was afraid to use a *tampon* because she was still a virgin."

***tear off a piece** (tɛər 'ɔːf ə 'piːs) verb phrase. vulgar. Have sexual intercourse.

teats (tiːts) noun, plural. 1. general use. An animal's mammary glands, such as a cow's or dog's. 2. vulgar. A woman's breasts.

testes ('tɛ stiːz) noun, plural. formal and medical use.
testicles ('tɛ stɪ kəlz) noun, plural. general use. Both of these terms mean the male reproductive glands located in the scrotum.

testosterone (tɛ 'stɑ stə roun) noun. formal and medical use. A male sex hormone.

that time of the month (ðæt taɪm əv ðə 'mʌnθ) noun phrase. euphemism. The monthly period. The time of menstruation.

(the) third sex (ðə 'θərd sɛks) noun. slang. Homosexual.

***throne** (θroun) noun. slang. The toilet.
(A throne is the official seat of a king or queen.)

***tinkle** ('tɪŋk əl) verb. children's word. Urinate.

titties ('tɪᴅ iːs) noun, plural. children's word and slang. The breasts.

tits (tɪts) noun, plural. slang. The breasts.

toilet ('tɔɪ lət) noun. general use. 1. The object that a person urinates or defecates into. It is located in the bathroom. 2. The bathroom itself.

toilet paper ('tɔɪ lət pei pər) noun. general use. A roll of soft tissue paper used in the bathroom.

toilet-train ('tɔɪ lət trein) verb. general use. To teach a young child to use the toilet. "Mrs. Murphy began to *toilet-train* her son when he was two and a half years old. In six months he was completely out of diapers." **toilet-trained** adjective. general use. No longer needing diapers. "Children must be *toilet trained* before they may attend most pre-schools."

toilet water ('tɔɪ lət wʌt ər) noun. general use. A light cologne (perfume) that is splashed on the body after a bath. (It is *not* water from the toilet!)

tokus ('tʊ kəs) also **tuchus** ('tʊ kəs) noun. euphemism. (from the Yiddish). The buttocks.

T

***tonsils** ('tɑn səlz) noun, plural. vulgar. A woman's breasts.

***tool** (tuːl) noun. vulgar. The penis.

topless ('tɑp ləs) adjective. general use. (said of a woman) Naked (with no clothes on) above the waist. "Yoshi went to a *topless* bar." (That is, where the waitresses were topless.) "*Topless* bathing suits are not allowed on most public beaches in New Jersey."

tough titty (tʌf 'tɪ ti) expression. vulgar. That's too bad, but it's all you deserve. Life is hard for all of us.

* words with additional meanings not listed

transvestite (trænz 'vɛs taɪt) also: **T.V.** noun. formal and general use. A person who loves to dress, make up, and appear as a person of the opposite sex. Both heterosexuals and homosexuals may be transvestites.

***trick** (trɪk) noun. slang. (used by prostitutes) A paid act of sexual intercourse. "She turned seven *tricks* Friday night."

tubal ligation ('tuː bəl laɪ 'gei ʃən) noun. formal and medical use. A surgical operation that prevents pregnancy. Sterilization of a woman. A fallopian tube is cut and tied so the ova (eggs) cannot go through it.

turd (təːrd) noun. vulgar. A piece of feces.

***turn the corner** (təːrn ðə 'kɔːr nər) verb phrase. slang. Make the decision to act out one's homosexuality by having a homosexual relationship.

***turn on** (təːrn 'ɑn) verb. slang. To excite someone sexually. "Some men know how to *turn a woman on*, and some men don't," she said.

***turned on** (təːrnd 'ɑn) adj. slang. Excited, aroused for sexual activity. "Disco music really *turns me on*," she said.

tush (tʊʃ) noun. euphemism and children's word. The buttocks. Also **tushie**.

twat (twɑt) noun. vulgar. The vagina.

U

Uncle Tom ('ʌŋk əl 'tɑm) noun. slang, derogatory. A black person who does not side with black people against white people.

undies ('ʌn diːz) noun, plural. euphemism. Underwear.

unmentionables (ʌn 'mɛn tʃən ə bəlz) noun, plural. euphemism. A woman's underwear.

unwell ('ʌn 'wɛl) adj. euphemism. Having one's menstrual period.

ureter (yuː 'riː tər) noun. formal and medical use. The tube that urine travels from the kidney to the bladder.

urethra (yuː 'riː θrə) noun. formal and medical use. The tube that goes from the bladder to exit the body. "Urine is formed in the kidneys, stored in the bladder, and passed out of the body through the *urethra*."

urinate ('yəːr ə neit) verb. formal. Pass (expel) waste liquid (urine) from the bladder; pee.

urinal ('yəːr ɛ nəl) noun. general use. A container or object that men can urinate into; a public toilet for men.

urine ('yəːr ɪn) noun. formal and general use. The waste liquid that is filtered out of the blood.

urogenital ('yəːr ou 'dʒɛ nə təl) adjective. formal. Referring to all the genital and urinary organs and functions.

urologist (yəːr 'ɑ lə dʒɪst) noun. formal. A doctor who specializes in treating problems involving the kidneys, bladder, penis, and testicles.

used-beer department ('yuːzd 'biər də 'pɑːrt mənt) noun phrase. slang. The bathroom in a tavern or barroom or any other place where people drink beer.

uterus ('yuː tə rəs) noun. formal and general use. The female organ in which a baby may grow. The *womb*.

V

V

VD (viː diː) noun. euphemism and general use. Venereal disease.

vaginismus (væ dʒɪ 'nɪz məs) noun. formal and medical use. A sudden cramping of muscles in the vagina. This happens when a young woman has many fears about sex. It can prevent intercourse. When it happens during sexual intercourse, the man may not be able to get his penis out until the woman is relaxed. Sometimes a doctor is needed to separate the two partners!

vasectomy (væ ˈsɛk tə mi) noun. formal. A surgical procedure to sterilize a man. The urologist (doctor) cuts a piece of the *vas deferens* in the testicle. The sperm can no longer travel out of the body through the penis.

venereal disease (və ˈni riː əl də ˈziːz) Also **VD**. noun. general use. This term refers to several different diseases that are spread by sexual contact. "Syphilis and gonorrhea are the two most common *venereal diseases*." "He went to a *VD* clinic to get a blood test for syphilis."

***vibrator** (ˈvaɪ breɪ tər) noun. general use. An electric-powered (or battery-powered) object used to provide sexual pleasure. A battery-powered *dildo*.

virgin (ˈvər dʒɪn) noun. general use. A woman or man who has not had sexual intercourse. "They were both *virgins* when they got married."

virginity (vər ˈdʒɪ nə ti) noun. general use. The state of being a virgin. "She lost her *virginity* many years before she got married."

the Virgin Mary (ðə ˈvər dʒɪn ˈmɛər i) noun. general use. 1. The mother of Jesus Christ. According to Christian teachings, Mary conceived Jesus without having sexual intercourse with any man. 2. A non-alcoholic drink: Tomato juice. (A *Bloody Mary* is tomato juice with vodka. "Bloody Mary" was a Catholic queen of England who ordered many non-Catholics killed.)

***virile** (ˈvi rəl) adj. formal and general use. 1. Manly. Having the ability to perform sexual intercourse. 2. Strong; brave.

virility (və ˈrɪ lə ti) noun. formal. The ability to perform sexual intercourse.

visit the sand box verb phrase. slang and euphemism. Go to the bathroom.

***void** (vɔɪd) verb. formal. Urinate.

voyeur (vɔɪ 'yər) noun. formal. A person who enjoys watching other people get undressed or have sexual intercourse. A "peeping Tom."

vulva ('vʌl və) noun. formal. The external female sexual parts, including the labia (lips), the entrance to the vagina, and the clitoris.

W

***warheads** ('wɑːr hɛdz) noun. slang, offensive. Large breasts that are revealed in a tight sweater. (Seeming like the pointed tips of missiles)

wash room ('wɑʃ ruːm) noun. euphemism. The toilet.

***water, to pass** ('wʌ ᴅər, tə pæs) verb phrase. euphemism. Urinate.

water the lilies ('wʌ ᴅər ðə 'lɪ liːz) verb phrase. slang. Urinate.

***watermelons** ('wʌ tər mɛ lənz) noun, plural. slang. A woman's (large) breasts.

water one's pony ('wʌ tər wʌnz 'pou ni) verb phrase. slang. Urinate.

***water sports** ('wʌ tər spɔːrts) noun, plural. slang. Urinating on one's partner during sexual play.

wax the cucumber ('wæks ðə 'kyu kʌm bər) verb phrase. slang. Masturbate.

wee wee ('wiː wiː) 1. verb. children's word. Urinate. 2. noun. children's word. Urine.

***well-endowed** ('wɛl en 'daʊd) adjective. slang. 1. (For a male) having a large penis. 2. (For a woman) having large breasts. Having been endowed with (given) a gift by nature or God.

***wet** (wɛt) 1. verb. euphemism. Urinate. "The baby *wet* his pants." 2. adj. slang. A sexually aroused woman gets *wet*. That is, her vagina becomes well-lubricated.

wet dream ('wɛt dri:m) noun. euphemism. A sexually exciting dream that results in ejaculation of semen during sleep. A nocturnal emission.

whack off (wæk 'ɔ:f) verb. vulgar. Masturbate.

whang (wæŋ), **whanger** noun. vulgar. The penis.

where the sun don't shine expression. slang. In the rectum. In the vagina.

***whore** (hɔ:r) noun. vulgar. A cheap prostitute. A women who charges money for an act of sexual intercourse.

whore house ('hɔ:r haʊs) noun. vulgar. A house of prostitution.

***wick** (wɪk) noun. slang. The penis. (A wick is the string in a candle.) To dip *one's wick* is to have sexual intercourse.

***wiener** ('wi:n ər) noun. slang and children's word. The penis. (Wiener is another word for *hot dog*.)

***withdrawal** (wɪθ 'drɔ əl) noun. general use. During intercourse, just before the moment of ejaculation, the mar tries to withdraw his penis from the vagina and ejaculate outside his partner, with the hopes of preventing pregnancy.

womb (wu:m) noun. general use. The uterus.

***woody** ('wʊd i) noun. slang. An erection.

***working girl** noun. slang. A prostitute.

X

X-rated ('ɛks 'reit id) adj. general use. Pornographic. Produced for the purpose of arousing sexual excitement. "They rented some *x-rated* videos." **XXX rated**. Same as X-rated.

X.Y.Z. (ɛks waɪː ziː) verb phrase. euphemism. **Examine Your Zipper!** (Your fly is open.) A "secret" code term to let another person know that his or her zipper is down.

Y

yank off ('yæŋk 'ɔːf) verb. vulgar. Masturbate.

you-know-what noun. euphemism. 1. Sex organ (usually penis). 2. Anus. "Shove it up your *you-know-what*!"

You know what you can do with it! exclamation. euphemism for "*Shove it up your ass.*" (I don't want it.)

you-know-where (yuː nou 'wɛər) adjective phrase. euphemism. 1. Penis, vagina, or anus, depending on the context of the sentence. 2. In the bedroom, or in the bed.

To the Teacher

In 1980, the first edition of *Dangerous English!* rocked the ESL teaching community, shocking some and relieving others. Many teachers immediately recognized that their teenage and adult international students needed a reference such as this. A few were aghast that such a book could be published, and loudly declared that newcomers had no need and no right to know the common names for their body parts, or the interesting activities of same.

Those who recognized that this was a book whose time had come still wondered whether to use it as a text in their classroom. Librarians wondered whether to stock it on their shelves. However, some courageous pioneers made it available to their students in a great variety of ways, taking into consideration the sensitivities of their classes, and administrative realities.

We tapped our own and those pioneers' experiences for this updated "suggestions for teachers." The discussion questions following each chapter reflect the areas of interest that students found fascinating.

One problem that occurred when *Dangerous English!* was stocked in reference libraries was that it quickly became "the most frequently stolen book." To prevent disappointment, either stock enough copies each year to replace the "walkaways," or help students order it for themselves by copying the order form in the back, or by providing Delta System's Toll-Free number: 1-800-323-8270.

Since our previous edition, there have been many changes in the use of vulgar language on TV and in the movies. Where once foul language was clearly unwelcome and censored out, it now gets broadcast into living rooms during even "children's hours." There are great debates about the use of foul language on the Internet, as well as offers for "live sex" that reach young children. The Supreme Court has preserved free speech, but middle America is greatly angered. At this writing, citizens' lobbies are looking for ways to shut off the smut so it won't be available to children.

When people are emotionally involved, they retain information. Words that have a "charge" are more easily learned than non-charged words. Most of your students will learn the concepts and expressions in this book with less effort and more involvement than any other content matter in English! Since 90% of the language presented is, in fact, "quite clean" *Dangerous English!* will accomplish miracles in assisting in language growth. And the other 10%—well, many students need that too, to defend themselves when they go off to the locker room.

High-school students need and want the information in *Dangerous English!* They are entitled to a guide to distinguish between the colorful and the off-color language used around them, as well as to dignified ways to speak about their bodies and its functions. To neglect this area is to let them fend on their own, which can cause them embarrassment and get them into trouble.

However, the climate for respectful teaching about dangerous language in most high schools is far from favorable. We advise you not to use this text on public-school property during school hours, or with students under eighteen years of age *without the consent and approval of your school administrator*. Consult with him or her to find appropriate ways of making the book available to the students without bringing the wrath of the righteous upon your head, or losing your job. Perhaps arranging for voluntary after-school classes taught by someone other than anyone whose job would be at risk would be a solution.

If you work with college students and adults, it is most likely a different story. We suggest four very simple tactics to smooth the way for using *Dangerous English!* as a text in your classroom.

1. This works in a large program: Pool two or more classes with an opposite-sex colleague. Then divide the large group on gender lines, separating men and women for several class sessions. Teach only those students of your own gender. Have an opposite-sex colleague teach the other students. Even if students are very forward-thinking and profess to be unembarrassed by discussion of dangerous terms in mixed company, you want to underscore through your own actions that this is still not the case in most parts of American society. In a small program where you are the only teacher, call in a guest teacher of the opposite sex. Divide your class, and do the same as previously described.

2. Give your students fair warning. Announce your plan along these lines: "Next week we will discuss language that might be embarrassing or offensive. If any of you think this will make you uncomfortable, see me after class today for a different assignment—one using the library. If you complete this other assignment, you won't be marked absent." (The teachers who have used this technique report that no one has ever taken the option to do an alternative assignment. But a few students in classes where there was *no choice* felt uncomfortable.)

   What if you are uncomfortable yourself?

   All the more reason your students need help. Be honest with them. Tell them that you are also uncomfortable talking about this language and invite guest teachers to come into your class to help handle it for you. And *you* be the one who goes to the library for an alternative assignment!

3. In some adult-education or university settings it might be possible to organize a specific class for the purpose of learning about the different levels of language including slang and vulgar English. That way, students have self-selected themselves. There is enough material for discussion and vocabulary learning for a five-week course that meets two hours a week. Supplement the text discussions with videos. Include videos containing medical terms (such as movies of *A Child Is Born*, *A Girl [Boy] Grows Up* type), and "R" movies of the "tough cop" variety, to include street language and fighting words. (Preferably view ones with some redeeming social value or artistic excellence.) Preview the movies so you can select short segments to watch in class. Or, give outside assignments.

4. As a minimal gesture, you can make students aware of both the book and the areas ripe for difficulty and embarrassment. Let them take responsibility for reading *Dangerous English!* on their own. Or you might give the class a brief synopsis of the content of the book, and provide order forms so students may order their own copies. You can, in fact, collect their money and order directly for them, saving them much of the cost of shipping and handling.

Different students come to this material with different needs. Some of them will urgently want to know the formal and medical terms, and their general use equivalents. These students include foreign resident doctors, nurses, and other hospital personnel. They will need to be able to understand the various words their patients may use for parts of their body, their functions, and their ailments. They need to be able to express their questions and recommendations with the kinds of terminology and pronunciation that will prove to be comprehensible to their patients.

Other groups want to be able to express themselves politely, and avoid embarrassing pronunciations. Those who are parents will want to know how to advise their children when children come home with new expressions learned on the street.

College youth may be particularly eager to fit in with their peers on sports teams or in dormitory bull sessions.

Those who take an interest in understanding culture and human psychology will be curious about the use of the different levels of words.

Before distributing books, show students the cover and ask, What do you think the title *Dangerous English!* means? What would *Dangerous Japanese* or *Dangerous Spanish* mean to you? What kinds of words would you put in a book of *Dangerous Words* in your own language? Elicit the kinds of topics that your students consider dangerous and write them on the chalkboard to compare later with the table of contents of *Dangerous English!*

Have students read the overview, "What Is Dangerous English?" Conduct a discussion to find out what their concerns are in this area of language. Use this to guide you in developing later lessons.

If you're working in a classroom you'll want to set up a respectful and scholarly approach to the topic, rather than a snickering, embarrassed approach. That doesn't mean you won't have a lot of fun or laugh much of the time. But the topic of language taboos is perfect for awakening students to the study of the *nature* of language as well as merely *learning* the language. These discussions will help you defend the class to those in society who would say that there is no place for this sort of material.

Let your students know your feelings about the words. Go ahead and confess your embarrassment if and when that's what you feel. Let them know that people vary in their reactions—and that's OK. The difference is that English-speakers have been *conditioned from childhood* to react in certain ways to the sounds of these dangerous terms. Their bodies will actually sweat more, and hearts race, when speaking taboo words in a place where such words are not permitted by public agreement. To your students, all new words will start out as ordinary sounds, without the physical taboo built in! This puts them in danger.

Caution your students to err on the side of prudery until they have become completely familiar with their social environment and are sure of the words' meanings, the public attitude towards those words, and what their audiences' reactions will be.

Elicit your students' stories of embarrassing moments with English. Tell any of your own.

Take some time to teach the use of the pronunciation guide. Check students' comprehension of the sounds, to be sure they are using the guide effectively.

Have students preread one or two short chapters before class. During class, clarify meanings in the text. Use the questions at the end of each chapter for discussion relating what is dangerous in English to what is dangerous in the students' own language. Allow for questions, answers, anecdotes, and jokes. Provide a model for pronunciation and intonation. If there are words you'd rather not say, have a colleague make a cassette recording that you can play in class. This helps you heighten the distinction that some of the words are improper for polite use. You can even walk out of the classroom while they are listening.

Focus on the interest areas that meet your student's needs.

If you want to become further educated in the linguistic arena of dangerous words in any language, consult:

Maledicta Press
Dr. Reinhold Aman
P.O. Box 14123
Santa Rosa, CA, 95402-6123
USA

Bibliography

Alford, Richard D. and William J. O'Donnell. "Linguistic Scale: Cussing and Euphemisms." *Maledicta: The International Journal of Verbal Aggression*, Dr. Reinhold Aman, Editor. Vol. 7, pp. 155-163 (1983) Maledicta Press.

Aman, Reinhold. "Offensive Language Via Computer." *Maledicta*, Vol. 8, p. 1.
—"Offensive Words in Dictionaries." Part II, Op. cit. Vol. 8, pp. 123-153; Part IV: Op. cit. Vol. 10, pp.126-35.
—"Words Can Kill: The Anatomy of a Murder." Op. cit. Vol 8, p. 5.

Ashley, Leonard R. N. "Dyke Diction: The Language of Lesbians." *Maledicta*, Vol. 6 (1982).

Axtell, Roger E. *Do's and Taboos of Using English Around the World*. Wiley, New York, 1995.

Boston Women's Health Collective. *Our Bodies, Our Selves*. Simon & Schuster, New York, 1979.

Burke, David. *Bleep! A Guide to Popular American Obscenities*. Optima Books, Los Angeles, 1993.

Clifton, Merritt. "How to Hate Thy Neighbor: A Guide to Racist Maledicta." *Maledicta*, Vol. 2, pp. 149-173 (1978).

Dalzell, Tom. *Flappers to Rappers: American Youth Slang*. Merriam-Webster, Springfield, MA, 1996.

Dunn, Jerry. *Idiom Savant*. Holt, New York, 1997.

Fine, Gary Allen. "Rude Words: Insults and Narration in Preadolescent Obscene Talk." *Maledicta*, Vol. 5, pp. 51-68 (1981).

French, Lawrence. "Racial and Ethnic Slurs: Regional Awareness and Variations." *Maledicta*, Vol. 4, (1980).

Green, Jonathan. *The Slang Thesaurus*. Penguin, New York, 1986

Hentoff, Nat. "The Deflowering of the American Heritage Dictionary." *Maledicta*, Vol. 7, pp. 121-128 (1983).

Herbst, Philip H. *The Color of Words: An Encyclopedic Dictionary of Ethnic Bias in the United States*. Intercultural Press, Yarmouth, ME, 1997.

Lutz, William. *Doublespeak*. Harper Perennial, New York, 1996.

Morris, William, ed. *The American Heritage Dictionary of The English Language*. Houghton Mifflin Co., Boston, 1976.

Preston, Dennis R. "Lusty Language Learning: Confessions on Acquiring Polish." *Maledicta*, Vol. 6, pp. 117-120 (1982).

Rawson, Hugh. *Wicked Words: a Treasury of Curses, Insults, Put Downs, and Other Formerly Unprintable Terms from Anglo Saxon Times to the Present*. Crown Trade Paperbacks, New York, 1989.

Spears, Richard A. *Slang and Euphemism: A Dictionary of Oaths, Curses, Insults, Ethnic Slurs, Sexual Slang, and Metaphors*, 2nd Edition. Signet Penguin, New York, 1991.

Terry, Roger L. "A Connotative Analysis of Synonyms for Sexual Intercourse." *Maledicta*, Vol. 7, pp. 237-252 (1983).

Wentworth, Harold and Stuart Berg Flexner, compilers/eds. *Dictionary of American Slang*, 2nd Supp. Edition. Thomas Y. Crowell Co., New York, 1975.

Wilson, Wayne J. "Five Years and 121 Dirty Words Later." *Maledicta*, Vol. 5, pp. 243-254 (1981).